921
ROW

Steffens, Bradley,
1955-

J.K. R

$32.45

921
ROW

Steffens,
Bradley,
1955-

J.K. Rowling.

3349003017184

$32.45

DATE	BORROWER'S NAME	
1-9-13	Luis Gonzalez	

J.K. Rowling

J.K. Rowling

by Bradley Steffens

LUCENT BOOKS

An imprint of Thomson Gale, a part of The Thomson Corporation

THOMSON
™
GALE

Detroit • New York • San Francisco
New Haven, Conn. • Waterville, Maine • London

For John, who first shared the magic of Harry Potter with me

LIBRARY OF CONGRESS CATALOGING-IN-PUBLICATION DATA

Steffens, Bradley, 1955–
J.K. Rowling / by Bradley Steffens.
    p. cm. -- (People in the news)
Includes bibliographical references and index.
ISBN-13: 978-1-59018-963-4 (alk. paper)
ISBN-10: 1-59018-963-9 (alk. paper)
1. Rowling, J. K.—Juvenile literature. 2. Authors, English—20th century—Biography—Juvenile literature. 3. Potter, Harry (Fictitious character)—Juvenile literature. 4. Children's stories—Authorship—Juvenile literature. I. Title.

PR6068.O93Z8875 2007
823'.914--dc22
[B]   2006018520

Printed in United States of America

Contents

Fame and celebrity are alluring. People are drawn to those who walk in fame's spotlight, whether they are known for great accomplishments or for notorious deeds. The lives of the famous pique public interest and attract attention, perhaps because their experiences seem in some ways so different from, yet in other ways so similar to, our own.

Newspapers, magazines, and television regularly capitalize on this fascination with celebrity by running profiles of famous people. For example, television programs such as *Entertainment Tonight* devote all of their programming to stories about entertainment and entertainers. Magazines such as *People* fill their pages with stories of the private lives of famous people. Even newspapers, newsmagazines, and television news frequently delve into the lives of well-known personalities. Despite the number of articles and programs, few provide more than a superficial glimpse at their subjects.

Lucent's People in the News series offers young readers a deeper look into the lives of today's news makers, the influences that have shaped them, and the impact they have had in their fields of endeavor and on other people's lives. The subjects of the series hail from many disciplines and walks of life. They include authors, musicians, athletes, political leaders, entertainers, entrepreneurs, and others who have made a mark on modern life and who, in many cases, will continue to do so for years to come.

These biographies are more than factual chronicles. Each book emphasizes the contributions, accomplishments, or deeds that have brought fame or notoriety to the individual and shows how that person has influenced modern life. Authors portray their subjects in a realistic, unsentimental light. For example, Bill Gates—the cofounder and chief executive officer of the software giant Microsoft—has been instrumental in making personal computers the most vital tool of the modern age. Few dispute his business savvy, his perseverance, or his technical expertise, yet critics say he is ruthless in his dealings with competitors and driven more by his desire to maintain Microsoft's dominance in the computer industry than by an interest in furthering technology.

In these books, young readers will encounter inspiring stories about real people who achieved success despite enormous obstacles. Oprah Winfrey—the most powerful, most watched, and wealthiest woman on television today—spent the first six years of her life in the care of her grandparents while her unwed mother sought work and a better life elsewhere. Her adolescence was colored by promiscuity, pregnancy at age fourteen, rape, and sexual abuse.

Each author documents and supports his or her work with an array of primary and secondary source quotations taken from diaries, letters, speeches, and interviews. All quotes are footnoted to show readers exactly how and where biographers derive their information and provide guidance for further research. The quotations enliven the text by giving readers eyewitness views of the life and accomplishments of each person covered in the People in the News series.

In addition, each book in the series includes photographs, annotated bibliographies, timelines, and comprehensive indexes. For both the casual reader and the student researcher, the People in the News series offers insight into the lives of today's news makers—people who shape the way we live, work, and play in the modern age.

The Return of the Written Word

According to a 2004 report by the National Endowment for the Arts (NEA), the number of adults who read literature declined 10 percent between 1982 and 2002, a drop that represents the loss of 20 million readers. Although adults may be reading less, children are reading more, according to other surveys. Some experts refer to this renewed interest in the written word as the "Harry Potter effect"—a reference to the popular series of books about a boy wizard by British author J.K. Rowling.

Researchers investigating the reading habits of young people have documented the Harry Potter effect. According to "The Kids and Family Reading Report," released in July 2006 by Yankelovich, a consumer tracking firm, and Scholastic, a media company, 60 percent of young people aged five to seventeen have read some or all of the Harry Potter books. More than half of the Harry Potter readers said they had not read for pleasure before encountering Rowling's series. Nearly two-thirds, 65 percent, believe their school performance has improved since they started reading the series. Their parents agree, with 76 percent saying that reading Harry Potter has helped their child do better in school.

Research conducted in Great Britain supports the American study. The Federation of Children's Book Groups in the United Kingdom has found that 84 percent of teachers say that the Harry Potter series has helped improve literacy among their students, with 67 percent saying the books have helped turn

J.K. Rowling, author of the celebrated Harry Potter series of books, accepts the award for Book of the Year in London in 2006.

nonreaders into readers. "The sheer pervasiveness of JK Rowling's books means Harry Potter will certainly have impacted on children's literacy levels,"[1] says Colin Harrison, a professor of literacy studies who contributed to the report.

Harrison is right about one thing: Rowling's books are everywhere. Since the publication of the first Harry Potter book in 1997, the series has sold more than 300 million copies worldwide. The vast majority of these books have been published in English, but the series has been translated into sixty-three other languages as well. Many of the books are owned by libraries, making the works available to millions more.

The success of the Harry Potter series has enriched Rowling beyond imagination. Royalties from the books and the series of

A young fan in a wizard costume eagerly begins **Harry Potter and the Half-Blood Prince,** *the sixth book in the series, at a midnight book sale.*

motion pictures based on them have made Rowling the first author to earn a billion dollars from his or her works. Along the way, J.K. Rowling has become a household name. Her picture has appeared in countless newspapers, books, and magazines. She has been interviewed on television and radio, and in Internet chats. On a crisp fall day in October 2000, more than fourteen thousand fans crowded into the SkyDome baseball stadium in Toronto, Canada, to hear her read from her books.

What is most remarkable is that these staggering accomplishments have been achieved one reader at a time. As *Time* magazine's Paul Gray observed, "Any assessment of her extraordinary impact should focus principally on the private transaction, as old as storytelling, between the speaker and the listener, or a more recent innovation, the writer and the reader. Here, in the hush of imagination, is where Rowling works her magic."[2]

Many of Rowling's readers have written back to her, revealing how their lives were touched by her words. In an essay submitted to Scholastic's "How the Harry Potter Books Changed My Life" contest, nine-year-old Tyler Walton, who suffers from leukemia, wrote, "I sometimes think of Harry Potter and me as being kind of alike. He was forced into situations he couldn't control and had to face an enemy that he didn't know if he could beat." Walton wrote that he draws strength from his fictional hero, adding, "Harry Potter helped me get through some really hard and scary times."[3]

Essays and letters like Walton's pour into the offices of Rowling, her agent, and her publishers every day. Such stories are the most dramatic examples of something that happens to a greater or lesser extent to all of Rowling's readers: They begin to sense that the world is filled with unseen possibilities and startling truths—a precious and mysterious place accessible through the most amazing portal of all, the human mind.

Chapter One

Growing Imagination

On a 500-mile (805km) train trip from King's Cross station in London, England, to a naval base in Arbroath, Scotland, Peter Rowling and Anne Volant had the kind of encounter sometimes described as magical: Volant said she was cold; Rowling offered her his coat. The two spoke and took an instant liking to one another. They had a lot in common. They were both eighteen years old and members of the Royal Navy. The nine-hour train trip flew by as the two young people traded stories about their lives. By the time they reached Arbroath, Rowling and Volant had decided to see each other again.

A few months after they met in 1964, Rowling and Volant left the Royal Navy. Volant was pregnant, and on March 14, 1965, she and Rowling married. Peter Rowling found work as an apprentice production engineer at the Bristol Siddeley aircraft engine factory in Bristol. Anne Rowling did not look for work outside the home. Instead, she prepared for the birth of her child.

Rustic Retreat

Rather than live in the city, the Rowlings settled in the small town of Yate, 10 miles (16km) northeast of Bristol. The Rowlings moved into a modest home at 109 Sundridge Park, a gently curving street not far from the Frome River. Anne and Peter Rowling enjoyed the rustic setting and often took walks around the neighborhood. Not far from the Rowlings' home stood Stanshawes Court, a three-story Victorian manor built in 1874. The massive stone building, now a hotel, overlooks the entrance to Kingsgate Park, a wooded area containing two small lakes that was once part of the manor's grounds. Also within walking distance of the Rowlings' home was Cottage Hospital, located at 240 Station Road. It was here that Anne Rowling gave birth to

J.K. Rowling poses for the press at a meeting in New York in 2000.

her first child, a girl, on July 31, 1965. The Rowlings named their baby Joanne.

Birth Certificate Controversies

Anne and Peter Rowling did not give their daughter a middle name—a fact that became a matter of controversy many years later when Joanne Rowling's first book appeared under the name J.K. Rowling. Rowling's publisher told the press that J.K. stood for Joanne Kathleen. For three years, reporters, authors, and interviewers repeated this story. In July 2000, however, a Bristol newspaper published a copy of Rowling's birth certificate, which shows that Rowling was not given a middle name. Richard Savill of the English newspaper the *Telegraph* described the initials as a marketing ploy dreamed up by Rowling's publishers to obscure the fact that Rowling is a woman, since many publishers believe that boys tend not to read books by female authors. Rowling confirmed the gist of Savill's story, adding that she and her publisher agreed that J. Rowling sounded too plain. She suggested using J.K., partly because K follows J in the alphabet, so the two letters sound good together, and partly because Rowling's grandmother was named Kathleen.

The lack of a middle name was not the only controversy to arise from Rowling's birth certificate. Fans and reporters were also surprised to learn that she was born in Cottage Hospital in Yate. In her online autobiography, *The Not Especially Fascinating Life So Far of J.K. Rowling*, the author wrote, "I was born in Chipping Sodbury General Hospital, which I think is appropriate for someone who collects funny names."[4]

Biographer Sean Smith reproduced Rowling's birth certificate in his book *J.K. Rowling: A Biography*, commenting, "Rowling was not actually born in Chipping Sodbury and never lived there."[5] A spokeswoman for Rowling said only that the author was furious that Smith had written an unauthorized biography and that she did not intend to read it. Since a birth certificate is a public record, Rowling would seem to have little reason to complain about its publication. Nor is it surprising that fans would wonder why she published the false account of her birthplace. It is possible, of course, that she never examined her birth certificate and that she made an honest mistake. It is also possible that she preferred Chipping Sodbury to Yate because it appealed to her love of odd names. Rowling has never commented on the matter.

Little Sister

On June 28, 1967, less than two years after giving birth to Joanne, Anne Rowling had a second child, this time at home. Joanne's earliest memory was of her sister's birth. "My dad gave me Play-Doh the day she arrived, to keep me occupied while he ran in and out of the bedroom," she recalls. "I have no memory of seeing the new baby, but I do remember eating the Play-Doh."[6]

The Rowlings named their second daughter Dianne. Because of the similarity of the names, Joanne and Dianne Rowling were almost always called by their nicknames, Jo and Di. The names Joanne and Dianne both contain the name Anne. The fact that the two daughters shared parts of their names with their mother and with each other was symbolic of the close relationship the three would have. Later, Jo reflected on how close she was to her mother, who was just twenty years old when she was born. "Because I was the older child, to me she was almost like an older sister," she told Matt Seaton, a reporter for the *Guardian* newspaper. "I was never in any doubt that she was my mum, but that kind of relationship was there."[7]

Jo also bonded with her little sister. They played together, watched cartoons together, and listened to stories their parents read to them. Anne and Peter Rowling were avid readers who exposed their children to books at an early age. "My most vivid memory of childhood is my father sitting and reading *Wind in the Willows* to me," Jo recalls. "I had measles at the time, very badly, but I don't remember that; I just remember the book."[8]

Rabbit Tales

Like many elder siblings, Jo took the lead in choosing what games she and Di played. She also made up stories that she told

This is an aerial view of the Frome River. J.K. Rowling spent her earliest years in Yate, a town near the river, by Bristol, England.

to her younger sister. Di asked to hear the stories over and over but complained whenever her sister changed them. To solve the problem, Jo began to write her stories down. "The first story I ever wrote down (when I was five or six) was about a rabbit called Rabbit," she recalls. "He got the measles and was visited by his friends, including a giant bee called Miss Bee." Jo enjoyed writing so much that she made a secret decision to pursue it as a career. "Ever since Rabbit and Miss Bee," she says, "I have wanted to be a writer, though I rarely told anyone so."[9]

Two years after Di was born, Peter and Anne Rowling bought their first home, a three-bedroom house at 35 Nicholls Lane in Winterbourne, a town not far from Yate. Several families lived on Nicholls Lane, including one with a name that would linger in Rowling's imagination for years—the Potters.

Graham and Ruby Potter had two children: Ian and Vicki. Ian Potter was no wizard, but he did have a great sense of humor and a flair for mischief. He once placed a slug on a plate and tried to convince Jo to eat it. Another time he tricked the Rowling girls into leaving their footprints in wet cement. The children often played outdoors, but according to Ian their favorite activity was dressing up. "Nine times out of ten," he later told *Book* magazine, "it would be Joanne who had the idea, and she'd always say, 'Can't we be witches and wizards?'"[10]

Tutshill

When Jo was nine years old, her family moved to the village of Tutshill, located in the Forest of Dean. It was here that Peter and Anne Rowling discovered an affordable home with a view of the Wye River. Peter Rowling had always wanted to fix up an older home, and got his wish when he and Anne found Church Cottage for sale. Built in 1848, the stone structure served as Tutshill's school until a larger school was built nearby in 1893. The Rowlings purchased Church Cottage and began to convert it into their dream home.

In the fall of 1974 Jo donned the uniform of Tutshill Church of England Primary School. Tutshill Primary was a small, old-fashioned school where the antique rolltop desks still had

Rowling Remembers Her Sister's Birth

On her official Web site, J.K. Rowling describes her memories of her sister's birth:

My sister Di arrived a year and eleven months after me. The day of her birth is my earliest memory, or my earliest datable memory, anyway. I distinctly remember playing with a bit of plasticine in the kitchen while my father rushed in and out of the room, hurrying backwards and forwards to my mother, who was giving birth in the bedroom. I know I didn't invent this memory because I checked the details later with my mother. I also have a vivid mental picture of walking into their bedroom a little while later, hand in hand with my father, and seeing my mother lying in bed in her nightdress next to my beaming sister, who is stark naked with a full head of hair and looks about five years old. Although I clearly pasted together this bizarre false memory out of bits of hearsay when I was a child, it is so vivid that it still comes to mind if I ever think about Di being born.

J.K. Rowling, "Biography," J.K. Rowling Official Site. www.jkrowling.com.

inkwells. There Jo met another person who would leave an impression on her: Mrs. Sylvia Morgan.

On Jo's first day at the new school, Morgan gave her a mathematics test to determine her academic rank. The test included fractions, which Jo had not yet learned. She did not get a single problem correct. Afterward, Morgan told Jo to sit at a desk on the right side of the class. Jo soon learned that Morgan assigned seats based on how intelligent she thought her students were. "The brightest sat on her left, and everyone she thought was dim sat on the right," she recalls. "I was as far right as you could get without sitting in the playground."[11]

Jo worked hard to prove she was smarter than her teacher thought she was. Her efforts paid off. "By the end of the year, I had been promoted to second left," she remembers, "but at a cost. Mrs. Morgan made me swap seats with my best friend, so that in one short walk across the room I became clever but unpopular."[12]

Aspiring Writer

Away from school, Jo spent much of her free time walking through the fields and along the Wye River with her sister. She also read for pleasure, delving into books intended for adults as well as those written for children. By the time she was nine, she was reading Ian Fleming's novels about the spy James Bond. She also began to read novels by the nineteenth-century English novelist Jane Austen, a keen observer of human behavior who often wrote about pairs of sisters coming of age. "My favorite writer is Jane Austen, and I've read all her books so many times I've lost count,"[13] Jo later disclosed in an interview. She also enjoyed C.S. Lewis's Narnia books, revealing a taste for fantasy.

Jo began to emulate the writers she loved, fashioning stories and creating characters with unusual names. She rarely shared her work with anyone other than Di, who was a constant source of encouragement. "My life's ambition has been to write full time," she later told *School Library Journal*. "This is all I have wanted from the age of six. I cannot overstate how much I wanted that. But I didn't talk about it at all. I just never really spoke about it, because I was embarrassed."[14]

Talented Teen

After graduating from Tutshill Primary School in 1976, Rowling started secondary school at Wyedean Comprehensive School. Surrounded by more mature students, the eleven-year-old Jo felt out of place. She also was experiencing the onset of puberty, which made her feel self-conscious. She later described herself during this time as, "a snotty, swotty [studious] little kid and very insecure."[15]

Despite her shortcomings, Jo made friends with other bookish students, whom she often entertained by telling stories.

"I used to tell my equally quiet and studious friends long serial stories at lunch-times," she remembers. "They usually involved us all doing heroic and daring deeds we certainly wouldn't have done in real life." Jo wrote some stories down, but mostly kept them to herself. "I wrote a lot in my teens, but I never showed any of it to my friends," she recalls, "except for funny stories that again featured us all in thinly disguised characters."[16]

Several of Jo's teachers noticed her writing ability and did their best to encourage the teenager to develop her creative talents. But Jo saw a different role for herself: She wanted to change the world for the better. She had become captivated by stories her great-aunt Ivy had told her about social activist Jessica Mitford. After reading Mitford's autobiography, *Hons and Rebels*, Rowling decided that she too would try to right the world's wrongs and work for social justice.

Illness in the Family

When Jo was fifteen, her mother was diagnosed with multiple sclerosis, a progressive disease of the central nervous system that can affect movement, vision, and sensation. The diagnosis came as a shock to the family, since Anne Rowling was only thirty-five years old. "She was so young and so fit," Jo remembers. "To have your body in rebellion against you is a dreadful thing to witness, let alone suffer."[17] At an age when children often rebel against their parents, Jo remained close with her mother.

Jo had only a few close friends at Wyedean Comprehensive. One of these was Seán P. F. Harris, a thoughtful young man who would remain one of Jo's best friends throughout her life. She did not own a car or know how to drive, but Seán did. Together they went to discos, concerts, and teenage hangouts in Bristol, Bath, and other large towns. Later, Jo would dedicate her second book to Seán, referring to him as her "getaway driver and foulweather friend."[18]

Growing Independence

Throughout her years at Wyedean, Jo continued to get good grades. Respected by classmates and teachers alike, she was

Jessica Mitford (seated) poses for a photo with her sister in the early 1920s. Mitford, a radical social activist, inspired the young Jo Rowling.

voted Head Girl in Year 11. In June 1983 seventeen-year-old Joanne Rowling graduated with honors.

Rather than take a year off from school, as is common in Britain, Jo enrolled in the University of Exeter the next fall. Unsure of what to study, she took her parents' advice and studied French. "This was a big mistake," she recalls. "I had listened too hard to my parents, who thought languages would lead to a great career as a bilingual secretary."[19]

Rowling may have regretted her course of study at Exeter, but while in college she learned valuable lessons about herself and the world around her. For the first time in her life, she began to make major decisions on her own. When the opportunity arose to study in France, she took it. The trip abroad added to her confidence. Not only did she study while in Paris, but she gained experience as a student teacher. While at Exeter, Rowling also fell in love, beginning a relationship that lasted for several years.

Rowling continued to write in her free time. She tried her hand at poetry, short stories, and drama. She even began a novel, which she nearly completed before abandoning it. This false start was far from a failure, however; she learned important lessons about plot, characterization, and dialogue. Rowling kept her writing to herself, showing it only to her boyfriend, Di, and a few others. Those closest to her encouraged her to share her talent with the world, but she believed her work was not ready for publication.

Cliff Top Drama

On her official Web site, Rowling recounts a game she used to play with her sister, Di:

We left the bungalow when I was four and moved to Winterbourne, also on the outskirts of Bristol. Now we lived in a semi-detached house with STAIRS, which prompted Di and I to re-enact, over and over again, a clifftop drama in which one of us would "dangle" from the topmost stair, holding hands with the other and pleading with them not to let go, offering all manner of bribery and blackmail, until falling to their "death." We found this endlessly amusing. I think the last time we played the cliff game was two Christmases ago; my nine-year-old daughter didn't find it nearly as funny as we did.

J.K. Rowling, "Biography," J.K. Rowling Official Site. www.jkrowling.com.

Important Places in
~ J.K. Rowling's Life ~

SCOTLAND

Aberdeen

North Sea

Edinburgh

IRELAND

Dublin ⊛

Manchester

NETHERLANDS

Atlantic
Ocean

Wye River

ENGLAND

Yate

Bristol

London

Exeter

Frome R.

BELGIUM

Paris ⊛

FRANCE

Bay of
Biscay

Oporto
PORTUGAL

SPAIN

Mediterranean
Sea

Working for Change

Rowling graduated with honors from Exeter in 1987 and moved to London. Inspired by Jessica Mitford, Rowling applied for a job with Amnesty International, a human rights watchdog group. Fluent in French, she was hired as a research assistant studying human rights abuses in French-speaking Africa. She used her lunch hours to begin work on a second novel.

At first, Rowling felt satisfied with her job at Amnesty International. She believed she was having a positive impact on the world. As time passed, though, she longed to work on the front lines of social change, but this was not possible for a newcomer. Disenchanted, she resigned from her job after two years.

Rowling landed several jobs as a bilingual secretary, but ended up leaving each one. "I had some office jobs, and anyone who worked with me will tell you that I was the most disorganized person that ever walked this earth," she later told an inter-

The Forest of Dean

During Joanne Rowling's teenage years, the Rowling family lived in Tutshill, a hamlet located in the Forest of Dean. Situated between the Severn and Wye rivers, the Forest of Dean consists of 35,000 acres (142 sq km) of both deciduous trees and conifers. One of the remaining royal forests in England, it was originally designated by the Saxons for hunting.

People born in the forest and whose parents were born in the forest are called foresters. The foresters have enjoyed special rights dating back to the Norman Conquest of 1066. The sheep keepers, known as sheep badgers, are free to simply turn their sheep out to graze. Foresters also are allowed to graze their pigs in the forest in the autumn months, where the animals feed on the acorns from the oak trees. Any forester who has worked in a mine for a year and a day may open up his own coal mine.

As a teenager, Rowling and her family lived in Tutshill, a village located in the Forest of Dean (pictured here) in Gloucestershire.

viewer. "I wasn't good. I'm *not* proud of that. I don't think it's charming and eccentric. I really should have been better at it, but I really am just all over the place when it comes to organizing myself."[20] She also abandoned her second novel.

Her career stalled, Rowling considered moving to Manchester, England's second-largest city, where her college boyfriend had settled. On weekends, she often took the train to Manchester to visit him. On one of these trips, in June 1990, the train back to London broke down in the middle of the English countryside. As she and the other passengers waited for the locomotive to be repaired, Rowling gazed out the window and began to daydream. Suddenly, in her mind's eye she saw a boy with dark hair, green eyes, glasses, and a mark on his forehead in the shape of a lightning bolt. Rowling did not yet know the young man's name, but she had just met Harry Potter.

Chapter Two

"It Was Like Research"

Stranded on a train between Manchester and London, Joanne Rowling imagined all kinds of things about the boy she had seen in her mind's eye. He was a wizard: not a full-fledged wizard, but a wizard in the making. He had powers, but he did not understand them. He would have to go through special training. Wizard training, at a school of witchcraft and wizardry. The trickle of ideas turned into a stream, then a torrent. Rowling searched for a working pen, but found none. She continued to daydream about the boy wizard until the train started moving again. For the remainder of the trip, Rowling tried to remember everything she could about the strange fantasy. "Rather than try to write it, I had to think it," she later recalled. "And I think that was a very good thing. I was besieged by a mass of detail, and if it didn't survive that journey, it probably wasn't worth remembering."[21]

Rowling realized all of her story ideas would not fit in one book, or even two. She envisioned the young wizard's saga as a seven-book series, one book for each year he would spend in school. The practical aspects of writing a seven-book series did not enter Rowling's mind. "When you dream, you can do what you like,"[22] she later said.

Creative Rush

When she got home, Rowling wrote down everything she could remember about the boy wizard and his adventures. She worked

A popular Christmas gift in 2000 was this Harry Potter puzzle with a special decoder magnifying glass. Harry Potter products became hugely popular.

in a frenzy of inspiration. "I had this physical reaction to it, this huge rush of adrenaline, which is always a sign that you've had a good idea," she says. "I'd had ideas I liked, but never quite so powerful. And Harry came first, in this huge rush. Doesn't know he's a wizard, how can he not know? And, very bizarrely, he had a mark on his forehead, but I didn't know why at that point. It was like research. It didn't feel as if I were entirely inventing it."[23]

Remembering the difficulties she encountered with her two unfinished novels, Rowling did not immediately start writing the first chapter of her imagined book. Instead, she made notes, sketched characters, and plotted the story. She reviewed the lists of names she had collected through the years, trying to match them up with the characters she created. She wanted to think the project through completely before she started writing.

Shortly after conceiving her story, Rowling moved to Manchester and took a clerical job with the Manchester Chamber of Commerce. She split her free time between the two men in her life—her boyfriend and the boy wizard she decided to name Harry Potter. Instead of spending her lunch hours with her coworkers, Rowling stole away to nearby cafés to work on her growing collection of notes and sketches.

Alternate World

At first Rowling gave little thought to the genre of story she was imagining. Wizardry simply offered Rowling a way to empower her young hero and allow him to escape from his stifling existence as the unwanted ward of his aunt and uncle. "There's a small part of you that wishes you could alter external things to be the way they ought to be," she observes. "That's why there will always, always, always be books about magic, discovering secret powers, stuff that you're not allowed to do."[24]

To support this story line, Rowling created a magical world that exists side by side with—and slightly overlaps—the world of ordinary human beings. Only after she filled this alternate world with enchanted characters and fantastic beasts did Rowling begin to realize what kind of book she was writing: "I was about two thirds of the way through, and I suddenly thought, 'This has got unicorns in it. I'm writing fantasy!'"[25]

Rowling knew that for the story to work, she would need to give her fictional world enough detail to make readers feel that they had stepped into a real place. Through the summer of 1990, she spent hours mapping out the school where Harry Potter would learn his craft:

> Hogwarts School of Witchcraft and Wizardry was the first thing I concentrated on. I was thinking of a place of great order, but immense danger, with children who had skill with which to overwhelm their teachers. Logically it had to be set in a secluded place, and pretty soon I settled on Scotland in my mind. I think it was a subconscious tribute to where my parents had married.[26]

The school emerged as an elaborate structure, several stories high, replete with enchanted staircases and secret passageways. Asked if she had sketched out a floor plan of Hogwarts to aid in her writing, Rowling replied, "I haven't drawn it, because it would be difficult for the most skilled architect to draw, owing to the fact that the staircases and the rooms keep moving. However, I have a very vivid image of what it looks like."[27]

Sound and Sense

The school and the characters within it all needed names, and Rowling proved especially adept at composing them. All her life Rowling had jotted down quaint, peculiar, or odd-sounding names she had seen on street signs, maps, war memorials, gravestones, and other places. The unusual hobby paid big dividends as the young writer attempted to populate her world. She plucked the name Hogwarts from a visit to a public garden. "I thought I made up Hogwarts," Rowling later said, "but recently a friend said, 'Remember we saw lilies in Kew Gardens.' Apparently there are lilies there called Hogwarts. I'd forgotten!"[28]

Although Rowling has claimed to have "a slight blind spot about poetry,"[29] she composed the names of her characters and places in her novels with a poet's sensitivity to sound and meaning.

Harriett Potter

In a radio interview on the Canadian Broadcasting Corporation's *This Morning Sunday Edition*, Rowling described a crisis she faced during the writing of *Harry Potter and the Philosopher's Stone* regarding the gender of her hero:

> I'd been writing about Harry for six months when I did suddenly stop and think, Hang on a moment. Why is he a boy?

> The simple answer is that's the way he came to me. A boy appeared in my brain—just this little scrawny, black-haired boy with glasses on. And so I wrote him, because he was the character who came to me.

> But I did stop and wonder. I did stop and think, Shouldn't it have been Harriett? And at that point it was too late. It was just too late, because Harry was too real to me as a boy. And Hermione was with me at this point, and I feel that Hermione is an absolutely indispensable part of the team. I love her as a character, and so I didn't change it. I wanted to go with my initial inspiration.

Quoted in CBC, "Interview: J.K. Rowling," *This Morning Sunday Edition*, October 23, 2000. http://radio.cbc.ca/programs/thismorning/sites/books/rowling_001023.html.

J.K. Rowling takes a break during a book signing at a New York City bookstore in 1999.

Rowling reads aloud to her fans at an event at Buckingham Palace in London.

She later told an interviewer how she came up with the name of a prominent wizard who is the author of many books:

> Gilderoy Lockhart is a good example. I knew his name had to have an impressive ring to it. I was looking through the *Dictionary of Phrase and Fable*—a great source for names— and came across Gilderoy, a handsome Scottish Highwayman. Exactly what I wanted. And then I found Lockhart on a war memorial to the First World War. The two together said everything I wanted about the character.[30]

Rowling sometimes used the root meanings of words to enrich her characters' names. For example, Dumbledore, the name of the headmaster at Hogwarts, is the Old English word for bumblebee. Rowling says the word "seemed to suit the headmaster, because one of his passions is music and I imagined him walking around humming to himself."[31]

Naming Lord Voldemort

Rowling drew on her knowledge of foreign languages to create distinctive names for other characters. For example, she conjured up the name of Lord Voldemort, the evil wizard who killed Harry Potter's parents, by combining two French words, *volonté* and *mort*. The meanings of the two French words emphasize traits of the villain: *Volonté* means "will" and *mort* means "death." In keeping with his name, Voldemort often seeks to impose his will on others, and he does not hesitate to kill those who oppose him.

Rowling's knowledge of Latin and Greek also seeped into her work. Critic Maureen Dowd observes,

> Rowling, who studied classics at the University of Exeter, chose names with a Latin ring: Lord Voldemort, Draco and Narcissa Malfoy, Albus Dumbledore, Nimbus 2000, Sibyll Trelawney. She came up with a Latin motto for the Hogwarts School: Draco Dormiens Nunquam Titillandus (Never Tickle a Sleeping Dragon). And she alludes to Cerberus and Orpheus with Fluffy, the three-headed, music-loving dog that guards the sorcerer's stone, and to Proteus with her shape-shifting animagus.[32]

Rowling borrowed the name of one her most important characters, Hermione Granger, from the works of the English poet and playwright William Shakespeare. "The first play I saw was at Stratford upon Avon," Rowling recalls. "We saw Shakespeare's *King Lear*. I was absolutely electrified by it. We also saw *The Winter's Tale* and that was where I found the name Hermione—although of course it didn't come in handy until years later."[33]

Not only did Rowling find names for her characters, but she also created detailed backgrounds for everyone, whether or not she would use the material in the book. "I almost always have complete histories for my characters," she later told an interviewer. "Sirius Black is a good example. I have a whole childhood worked out for him. The readers don't need to know that but I do. I need to know more than them because I'm the one moving the characters across the page."[34]

Rowling modeled some characters after people she knew. To create Harry Potter's close friend Ron Weasley, Rowling borrowed traits from her school chum Seán Harris. "Ron Weasley isn't a living portrait of Seán, but he really is very Seán-ish,"[35] Rowling says. Like Weasley, Harris always proved to be a loyal friend.

Rowling reached even further back in her life for a model for Professor Snape, the Potion Master who picks on Harry Potter in class. Recalling her menacing primary-school teacher Mrs. Morgan, Rowling told an interviewer, "There are a number of people who influenced the character of Snape in my books, and that teacher was definitely one of them."[36]

Hermione/Herself

As Rowling pondered her cast of characters, she decided her young wizard's inner circle of friends should include at least one girl his own age. Rowling did not have to look outside herself for inspiration for this character, whom she named Hermione Granger. "Hermione was very easy to create because she is based almost entirely on myself at the age of 11," Rowling later told an interviewer. "Like Hermione, I was obsessed with achieving academically, but this masked a huge insecurity. I think it is very common for plain young girls to feel this way." Hermione is passionate about individual rights, calling for the fair treatment of house elves, just as Rowling was inspired by Jessica Mitford to become a social activist. Rowling insists that at some point the similarities between her and Hermione end and exaggeration takes over. "She really is a caricature of me. I wasn't as clever as she is, nor do I think I was quite such a know-it-all, though former classmates might disagree."[37]

While Rowling has no trouble identifying the inspiration for Hermione Granger, she is hard-pressed to do the same for the black-haired boy with glasses who appeared in her mind during that fateful train ride from Manchester to London in June 1990. Rowling admits that she borrowed her hero's surname from her childhood friends Ian and Vicki Potter. "Harry is one of my favorite boy's names," Rowling says. "But he had several different surnames before I chose Potter. Potter was the name of a brother and sister who I played with when I was very young. We were part of the same gang and I always liked that surname."[38] Rowling dismisses the idea that Ian was an inspiration for Harry, however. With his outgoing personality and love of pranks, Ian seems to have more in common with the Weasley twins than he does with Harry.

Rowling's Greatest Fear

In a 2006 interview with Geordie Greig of *Tatler* magazine, J.K. Rowling discussed the impact her mother's death had on her books. "Death is the key to understanding J.K. Rowling," Greig wrote. "Her greatest fear—and she is completely unhesitant about this—is of someone she loves dying." Rowling told Greig: "My books are largely about death. They open with the death of Harry's parents. There is Voldemort's obsession with conquering death and his quest for immortality at any price, the goal of anyone with magic. So I understand why Voldemort wants to conquer death. We're all frightened of it."

Quoted in Geordie Greig, "Special JK," *Tatler*, February 2006, p. 130.

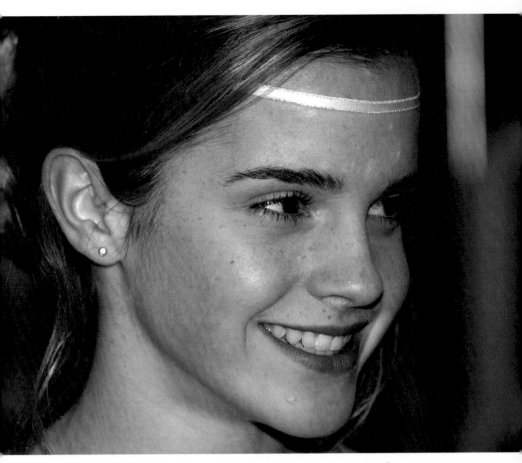

Emma Watson, who portrays Hermione Granger in the Harry Potter movies, arrives at the London premiere of Harry Potter and the Goblet of Fire in 2005.

Harry Potter has a quiet, serious side reminiscent of Rowling herself. Both the character and his creator share the same birthday —July 31. In addition, Harry wears glasses similar to the "very thick . . . glasses that were like bottle bottoms"[39] that Rowling said she wore as a child.

In *Harry Potter and the Sorcerer's Stone*, Rowling reveals that Harry Potter's cousin Dudley had punched Harry in the nose and broken his glasses. Rowling knew what it was like to be on the receiving end of a bully's abuse. While a student at Wyedean, Rowling was attacked by another girl. To the girl's surprise,

Rowling fought back. Harry Potter also refuses to be pushed around. "I admire bravery above almost every other characteristic," Rowling once said. "Bravery is a very glamorous virtue, but I'm talking about bravery in all sorts of places. It was brave of Harry to answer back to the Dursleys; they had all the cards, and he was standing up for himself even then. That's why I love him so much. He's a fighter."[40]

Harry Potter is not a clone of Rowling, though. A natural at flying a broomstick, Harry excels at the wizard's game Quidditch. Rowling, by contrast, broke her arm playing a game called netball. "Sport is such an important part of school life," Rowling says. "I am terrible at all sports, but I gave my hero a talent I'd love to have."[41]

Toward the end of 1990, Rowling had roughed out the plot of her seven-book series and began drafting the first novel. As the story took shape, Rowling remained convinced that the concept was strong. "The idea that we could have a child who escapes from the confines of the adult world and goes somewhere where he has power, both literally and metaphorically, really appealed to me,"[42] she later said. Despite her own excitement, however, Rowling worried that others might not think the concept was that good. As she headed home to Tutshill for Christmas, Rowling decided that she would not yet tell anyone in her family about Harry Potter.

Unexpected Loss

When Rowling returned to Church Cottage to spend the Christmas holidays with her family, she was struck by her mother's frail appearance. Anne Rowling was losing her battle with multiple sclerosis. "Her mobility was very limited; she looked ill, very ill—which I'd never really seen before. She was absolutely exhausted,"[43] Rowling says. Even so, she did not grasp the seriousness of her mother's condition.

On Christmas Eve, Rowling said good-bye to her parents and left to spend the remainder of the holidays with her boyfriend and his family. It was "the first time I had ever spent Christmas away from home," she recalls. A week later, she was celebrating New Year's Eve with her boyfriend and his family.

"I had gone to bed early, ostensibly to watch *The Man Who Would Be King*, but instead I started writing,"[44] Rowling later told Geordie Greig of *Tatler* magazine. She worked on the novel a long time before going to sleep. The next morning, she was awakened by a phone call:

> Dad called me at seven o'clock the next morning and I just knew what had happened before he spoke. I just knew. There was no way my father would call me at 7AM for any reason other than that. As I ran downstairs I had that kind of white-noise panic in my head but could not grasp the enormity of my mother having died.[45]

Rowling speaks during a television interview in 2005. Rowling was deeply affected by her mother's early death.

Rowling and her boyfriend immediately got in a car and drove back to Tutshill. "I was alternately a wreck and then in total denial," Rowling remembers. "At some point on the car journey I can remember thinking, 'Let's pretend it hasn't happened,' because that was a way to get through the next 10 minutes."[46]

Rowling blamed herself for not noticing that her mother was near death. If she had been more sensitive to her mother's condition, she might not have left to spend New Year's with her boyfriend. "I had no idea that MS would hit her so quickly," she later admitted. "And I wasn't there. That stirs up such guilt."[47]

If she could live her mother's last week over again, she would have told her about her new novel. "I know I was writing Harry Potter at the moment my mother died," Rowling recalls. "I had never told her about Harry Potter."[48]

The unexpected death of her mother had a profound effect on Rowling and on the book she was writing. "Her death depth-charged me," the author later observed. "It changed my life."[49] The loss infused Rowling's novels with new seriousness, depth, and power. Had her mother lived, the books might have taken a different direction. Without the lurking presence of death, they might have lacked emotional impact. In that sense, Anne Rowling's death was her final gift to her daughter. Her death brought Harry Potter to life.

Chapter Three

The Magic of Motherhood

Anne Rowling's death left a hole in her daughter's life. Joanne Rowling realized how close she had been to her mother and how much she had taken their relationship for granted. She also understood how fragile human existence is and how short it can be. She was anxious to fill the void left by her mother's death with love, family, and a sense of belonging. This desperation drove Rowling to make a series of dramatic life decisions.

Shortly after her mother's death, Rowling lost her job at the Manchester Chamber of Commerce. She took a position at the University of Manchester, but was not happy there. Her relationship with her boyfriend was also falling apart. In a final blow, thieves broke into her home and took her most valued possessions. "We were burgled, and everything my mother had left me was stolen," Rowling recalls. She was devastated. "People were incredibly kind and friendly, but I decided that I wanted to get away."[50]

Scanning the newspaper, Rowling came across an advertisement seeking English teachers for a school located in Oporto, Portugal. Remembering how she had enjoyed teaching English in Paris, Rowling applied for the position. The man who placed the ad, Steve Cassidy, the principal of the Encounter English Schools in Oporto, interviewed Rowling at a hotel near the railway station in Leeds. "We had coffee and chatted," Cassidy remembers. "She wasn't an outstanding candidate, but I thought she would be OK. She was a bit shy and I remember she looked a bit sad at the station. I think her mother had recently died."[51]

Rowling packed her things—including her Harry Potter note-books—and flew to Oporto in November 1991. Cassidy met Rowling at the airport and drove her to a four-bedroom apartment she would share with two other new teachers, Aine Keily and Jill Prewett. Like Rowling, Keily and Prewett were single, in their twenties, and hailed from the British Isles. Besides living and working together, the three also shared a social life, visiting Oporto's nightspots.

During a press conference in 2000, a thoughtful Rowling recalls her life and brief marriage in Portugal.

Love and Loss

In March 1992 the friends went to a local club called Meia Cava. The arrival of the young women caught the eye of a Portuguese journalism student named Jorge Arantes. He was particularly struck by Rowling's Celtic good looks. "This girl with the most amazing blue eyes walked in,"[52] Arantes remembers.

Fluent in English, Arantes began to speak with the young women. Soon he and Rowling were engrossed in conversation. Rowling mentioned she was rereading Jane Austen's *Sense and Sensibility*, a book Arantes had read. The fact that Arantes could talk about Rowling's favorite author made a good impression on the young English teacher.

Rowling and Arantes began to date, fell in love, and within a few weeks decided to live together. Rowling soon became pregnant. She and Arantes planned a trip to England to share the good news with her family. Before they could leave, however, Rowling suffered a miscarriage. The loss brought the two closer together. "We decided that when the time was right, we would try for another baby and also get married,"[53] Arantes recalls.

A Family of Her Own

Arantes proposed to Rowling shortly after the miscarriage, and she accepted. The couple announced their plans to friends and family. Dianne Rowling and her boyfriend, Roger Moore, flew to Portugal for the wedding. On Friday, October 16, 1992, Rowling and Arantes exchanged marriage vows at the civil registry office in Oporto.

Rowling shared her hopes and dreams with her new husband. She told him about Harry Potter and showed him the manuscript. "It was obvious to me straight away that this was the work of a genius," Arantes later told Dennis Rice of the *Daily Express*. "I can still remember telling Joanne, 'Whoa! I am in love with a great, great writer.'"[54]

Within a few weeks, Rowling was pregnant again. She continued to teach, even though she feared another miscarriage. This time, however, the pregnancy went well. On July 27, 1993, Rowling gave birth to a healthy baby girl, an event Rowling would later call "without doubt the best moment of my life."[55] Rowling and Arantes named their baby Jessica, after Jessica Mitford.

Shattered Dream

Arantes was out of work when Jessica was born. Faced with financial problems and the stress of caring for an infant daughter, Rowling and Arantes quarreled. On November 17, 1993, the couple's frustrations erupted into a terrible fight. Rowling told Arantes she no longer loved him. Hurt and angry, Arantes slapped Rowling,

The historic seaport city of Oporto, Portugal (shown here), was home to Rowling and her first husband. Her eldest daughter was born here.

forced her out of their home, and locked the door. Alone in the street, Rowling knew her marriage was over. She decided to leave Portugal immediately. She resigned from her teaching post, and within two weeks she and Jessica boarded a plane for England.

New Beginnings

Glad to be back in her native land, Rowling nevertheless felt out of place in London. She did not want to impose on her old friends, most of whom were single and carefree. Nor did she want to impose on her father, who had recently remarried. Rowling decided to phone her sister, who had married Roger Moore in September 1993 and moved to Edinburgh, Scotland, where Moore owned a restaurant. Di convinced Rowling to come to Edinburgh for Christmas.

Once in Edinburgh, Rowling pondered her next move. She was guided by her determination to give Jessica the kind of secure home her parents had given her. She decided Edinburgh

Why Rowling Divorced

J.K. Rowling is a private person who bristles at any intrusion into her privacy. After she became famous, her ex-husband sold a British newspaper his account of their years together. Reporters demanded to know Rowling's side of the story. She finally relented, telling Ann Treneman of the *Times* (London):

Obviously you do not leave a marriage after that very short period of time unless there are serious problems. I'm not the kind of person who bails out without there being serious problems. My relationship before that lasted seven years. I'm a long-term girl. And I had a baby with this man. But it didn't work. And it was clear to me that it was time to go, and so I went.

Quoted in Ann Treneman, "J.K. Rowling, the Interview," *Times* (London), June 30, 2000, p. 3.

was a good place to start. "Edinburgh is beautiful," she later explained, "has good public transport and did have, then, free museums, and I thought, 'I'll have a much better life here on a low income with my daughter.' I could just see that broke single-parenthood here would be easier."[56]

Rowling's plan was to teach again, but she discovered that her degree from Exeter and her teaching experience in Portugal did not qualify her to teach in Scotland. Without a job, Rowling applied for welfare, a process she found demeaning. "You have to be interviewed and explain to a lot of strangers how you came to be penniless and the sole carer of your child," Rowling recalls. "I know that nobody was setting out to make me feel humiliated and worthless, though that is exactly how I felt."[57]

Low Point

Rowling's application was approved, and early in 1994 she began to receive £69 ($103.50) a week for support. On her limited budget, Rowling could afford only a run-down apartment at 28 Gardiner Terrace in Edinburgh. Shortly after moving in, Rowling discovered that she and Jessica were not alone: A family of mice was living in the walls. "I never expected to mess up so badly that I would find myself in [a] . . . mouse-infested flat, looking after my daughter," she remembers. "And I was angry because I felt I was letting her down."[58]

Unable to afford to move out on her own, Rowling appealed to longtime friend Seán Harris for help. He gave Rowling the money she needed to move into a one-bedroom flat at 7 South Lorne Place in Leith, the old port area of Edinburgh. The move did not bring Rowling the security and peace of mind she sought, however. "A group of local boys amused themselves on dull nights by throwing stones at my two-year-old's bedroom window," she later wrote. A drunk once tried to force his way into her apartment, but Rowling was able to shove him back into the hall. Another time, Rowling was not as fortunate: A burglar broke in while she and Jessica were in bed. "Violence, crime and addiction were part of everyday life in that part of Edinburgh,"[59] she remembers.

Rowling felt frustrated at her inability to provide for Jessica. She once visited a friend who had a baby boy named Thomas. The visit turned into a nightmare. "I saw Thomas's bedroom full of toys and at that point, when I packed Jessica's toys away, they fitted into a shoe box, literally," Rowling recalls. Ashamed that she could not provide more playthings for her daughter, Rowling broke down. "I came home and cried my eyes out,"[60] she says.

An Escape

For comfort during these difficult times, Rowling turned to her sister, Di. During one visit, Rowling mentioned that she was working on a new book. As when they were young, Di wanted to know more about the story. Rowling let her sister read the first three chapters of her novel about Harry Potter. Rowling knew that her sister's opinion—good or bad—would mean a lot to her. A few pages into the book, Di laughed out loud. "It's possible that if she hadn't laughed, I would have set the whole thing on one side [abandoned the project],"[61] Rowling later said.

Encouraged by her sister's reaction, Rowling decided to finish the novel. If nothing came of the book, she at least would know that she had seen the project through. She found it was nearly impossible to write while Jessica was awake. To be productive, Rowling devised a special writing routine:

> I had to make full use of all the time that my then-baby daughter slept. This meant writing in the evenings and during nap times. I used to put her into the pushchair [stroller] and walk her around Edinburgh, wait until she nodded off, and then hurry to a café and write as fast as I could. It's amazing how much you can get done when you know you have very limited time.[62]

One of her favorite places to write was Nicolson's Café, an establishment co-owned by Rowling's brother-in-law. With yellow and blue cloths covering the tables and prints by the French artist Henri Matisse dotting the walls, Nicolson's had a cheerful atmosphere that appealed to Rowling. "She was quite an odd

Rowling attends the 2005 unveiling of a three-dimensional portrait of herself at the National Portrait Gallery in London.

sight," remembers Dougal McBride, Moore's business partner. "She would just push the pram with one hand and write away."[63]

As she worked, Rowling did not concern herself with who would read her book or how it would be marketed. "I wasn't really aware that it was a children's book," she later said. "I really wrote it for me, about what I found funny, what I liked."[64]

Just as Rowling was settling into a stable writing routine, she received word that her estranged husband had shown up in town, looking for her and Jessica. Fearing Arantes, Rowling obtained a type of restraining order against him. He left the country, but his visit convinced Rowling to file for divorce.

"A Push to Finish"

At the same time she was working on her book, Rowling pursued a teaching position. She found that to obtain a teaching credential, she had to complete a yearlong course. In January 1995 Rowling applied for one of the thirty openings in a program at Heriot-Watt University. To her relief, she was accepted. "We were never going to be rich if I had been a teacher, but we were never going to be dirt poor,"[65] she later said.

With the start of school approaching, Rowling hurried to complete her book. "I knew that unless I made a push to finish the first book now, I might never finish it," Rowling recalls. "I made a huge, superhuman effort."[66] By the time classes began, Rowling had finished a rough draft of the book, which she had titled *Harry Potter and the Philosopher's Stone*. Late in 1995 she began to type the manuscript on a manual typewriter. With little money to spend on photocopies, Rowling typed out two complete copies of the manuscript to submit to agents and publishers.

Not sure what to do next, Rowling visited the Edinburgh Central Library and looked through a copy of *Writers' & Artists' Yearbook* to find publishers and authors' agents that might be interested in what she called her "quirky little book."[67]

Amateur Mistakes

As she prepared to submit her manuscript, Rowling made many mistakes. First, her manuscript was two to three times longer than most publishers' guidelines recommended. Second, she put her synopsis and three sample chapters in a black plastic binder despite the fact that nearly all publishers and agents state that manuscripts should not be bound. Third, she included drawings with her work. Unless the author is also a professional illustrator, publishers do not want to see pictures with a manuscript. Finally, and most importantly, she submitted her work to an agency that did not represent children's authors. Because of these amateur mistakes, most publishers and agents would have rejected the manuscript without even reading it. This is exactly what Christopher Little's personal assistant and office manager, Bryony Evens, planned to do with *Harry Potter and the Philosopher's Stone*. "There would be no point in showing it to Chris if we didn't deal with it anyway,"[68] Evens later said.

Rowling, the highest-paid author of all time, receives an honorary degree at a college in Aberdeen, Scotland, in 2006.

Christopher Little, the literary agent willing to take a chance on Rowling and her first book, smiles at a Harry Potter display.

Fortunately for Rowling, Evens was not a typical manuscript screener. Just twenty-five years old, Evens had a youthful curiosity about the books submitted to the agency. The day Rowling's sample chapters arrived, Evens spent her lunch hour looking at the manuscripts she had set aside for rejection. She lingered over Rowling's submission. "I read the first page and thought it was really good,"[69] she recalls.

Instead of mailing the sample chapters back to Rowling, Evens set the manuscript aside and read it later. "The main thing that struck me, because I loved it, was the humor,"[70] Evens remembers. Even though it was not her job to discover authors, Evens decided to tell her boss about the manuscript. Impressed by the opening chapters, Little told Evens to request the complete manuscript.

The First Acceptance

When Rowling found a letter from the Christopher Little Literary Agency in her mailbox, she was not particularly excited. She had already received a rejection note from one literary agency and one publisher. She braced herself for another. "I assumed it was a rejection note," she recalls, "but inside the envelope there was a letter saying, 'Thank you. We would be pleased to receive the balance of your manuscript on an exclusive basis.'" Six years had passed since Harry Potter had first appeared in Rowling's imagination. She had spent countless hours developing his personality, creating his friends and enemies, devising dangers and narrow escapes. Now, for the first time, someone outside her family was showing an interest in his world. "I could not believe it," she later said. "I read it eight times."[71]

Rowling sent the remainder of the manuscript to Christopher Little immediately. Evens was the first to read it. "When it came I just couldn't put it down," she says. "I remember making a mental list of what was great about it—it had a school story, the orphan with an evil stepfamily, lots of witches, wizards, a really good detective story with a twist at the end of the story."[72]

Evens passed the manuscript to Little with a strong recommendation. As Little left the office that evening, he took the manuscript with him. Later that night he read the typed pages. He returned to the office the next morning and congratulated Evens on her find. They wrote to Rowling, asking her to make minor revisions. Rowling welcomed the agent's suggestions and quickly made the requested changes. Pleased with the result, Little offered Rowling a standard contract, and she accepted it.

Culmination

The Christopher Little Agency began sending the manuscript around to various children's publishers. One by one, the submissions were returned. As the manuscripts came back, Evens sent them out to other publishers. Twelve publishers passed on the opportunity to publish *Harry Potter and the Philosopher's Stone* before Evens slipped the manuscript into an envelope addressed to Bloomsbury Publishing.

Barry Cunningham, who headed the publisher's new children's division, was the first person at Bloomsbury to read Rowl-

---

Godmothers of Swing

When J.K. Rowling completed her third book, *Harry Potter and the Prisoner of Azkaban*, she honored her former Oporto roommates with the cryptic dedication, "To Jill Prewett and Aine Keily, the Godmothers of Swing." Many readers wondered about the meaning of the nickname Rowling gave to her friends. Many assumed that Prewett and Keily must have shared an interest in swing music, the jazzy dance music popularized in the 1940s by big band leaders such as Benny Goodman, Glenn Miller, and Duke Ellington, or the fast-paced dances performed with the music. In fact, the nickname arose from the name of a popular Oporto discotheque, Swing, which the three women often visited to socialize, dance, and listen to music.

J.K. Rowling, *Harry Potter and the Prisoner of Azkaban*. New York: Scholastic, 1999, p. iv.

ing's manuscript. "It was just terribly exciting," Cunningham remembers. "What struck me first was that the book came with a fully imagined world. There was a complete sense of Jo knowing the characters and what would happen to them."[73] Bloomsbury offered Rowling a £1,500 ($2,250) advance against royalties for the right to publish the book.

Little called his client to give her the good news. Rowling was thrilled. "Nothing since has matched the moment when I actually realized that 'Harry' was going to be published," Rowling later said. "That was the realization of my life's ambition—to be a published author—and the culmination of so much effort on my part. The mere fact that I would see my book on a bookshelf in a bookshop made me happier than I can say."[74]

Chapter Four

Miraculous Success

In 1997 more than one hundred thousand books were published in the United Kingdom. The chances of any of them becoming a best seller were slim at best—least of all, perhaps, a children's book by an unknown writer with an initial print run of five hundred copies. No one was more aware of this fact than Joanne Rowling. "I had been very realistic about the likelihood of making a living out of writing children's books—I knew it was exceptionally rare for anybody to do it—and that didn't worry me," she remembers. "I prayed that I would make just enough money to justify continuing to write, because I am supporting my daughter single-handedly."[75] Her prayers were answered. Within a month of its publication, Rowling's first book became one of the best-selling books in the United Kingdom.

Success did not come overnight, however. It was more than a year from the time her book was accepted by Bloomsbury before it appeared in her local bookshop. In the meantime, Rowling had to support herself and her daughter and somehow find time to continue telling the story of Harry Potter and his Hogwarts friends.

Leith Academy

Rowling received two advance payments from Bloomsbury, but it was not enough money to change her plans about becoming a teacher. Rowling studied hard and graduated from the teaching program in July 1996. She registered as a substitute teacher with the General Teaching Council, Rowling landed a part-time teaching job at Leith Academy, a school located just 600 yards (559m) from her front door. Best of all for Rowling, the school housed an on-site day care center, where she could place Jessica while she taught.

A picture of the first Harry Potter book in the United States reflects its new title, changed to accommodate American readers.

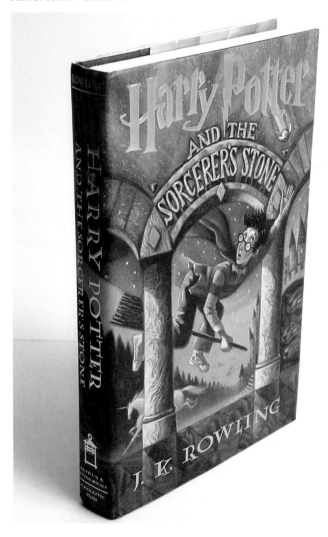

Rowling did not want other teachers or administrators to view her as anything but a dedicated teacher, so she kept her writing career a secret. The truth almost got out, however, when Rowling sent a student named Maggie to her desk to get some paper. As she did so, Maggie noticed some manuscript pages lying about. "She was ages at the desk," Rowling later told the *Guardian*, "and I turned round and said, 'Maggie will you come back and sit down,' and she went 'Miss, are you a writer?' I think I said, 'No it's just a hobby.'"[76]

It soon became much more than that. Rowling applied for a writer's grant from the Scottish Arts Council to help supplement her income. Only residents of Scotland who had already published a book were eligible to apply for the grant. Although Rowling's first book was not yet out, the council agreed to consider her proposal. After reading a few chapters of *Harry Potter and the Philosopher's Stone*, the council's literary director, Jenny Brown, recommended Rowling for an award. The council awarded her £8,000 ($12,000)—more than five times her advance from Bloomsbury.

The first thing Rowling did after receiving her grant was buy a computer so she could revise her manuscripts as she typed. The computer did not change her method of composition, however. She continued to draft her manuscripts by hand.

Because she had mapped the plots for the entire series, Rowling was able to write the second installment, *Harry Potter and the Chamber of Secrets*, quickly. She shipped her second manuscript off to Christopher Little in July 1997, one week after her first book came off the press.

"An Extraordinary Moment"

Rowling once said that her "wildest fantasies hadn't gone much further than the book being published and the pinnacle of achievement seemed to me to be a review in a quality newspaper."[77] She realized the first of her lifelong ambitions on June 26, 1997, when Bloomsbury released the first edition of *Harry Potter and the Philosopher's Stone*.

When Rowling saw the book and held it in her hands, she felt giddy with pride. "I walked around all day with a finished copy tucked under my arm," she told biographer Lindsey Fraser. "The first time I saw it in a bookshop I had this mad desire to sign it. It was an extraordinary moment."[78]

Not long after achieving her first goal, Rowling reached her second. A short review appeared in the *Scotsman*, an Edinburgh newspaper, that hailed *Harry Potter and the Philosopher's Stone* for making "an unassailable stand for the power of fresh, innovative story-telling in the face of formula horror and sickly romance."[79]

While it was helpful to receive a glowing notice from the local newspaper, a more important review appeared in the *Sunday Times* of London, a newspaper read throughout the United Kingdom. Reviewer Nicolette Jones favorably compared Rowling's work to that of best-selling author Roald Dahl. "Not yet as well known as Philip Ridley or Robert Swindells, but surely destined to be, is J K Rowling, whose first children's book, *Harry Potter and the Philosopher's Stone*, is already winning accolades and prizes," wrote Jones. "This is a story full of surprises and jokes; comparisons with Dahl are, this time, justified."[80]

Spectacular Bids

Three days after *Harry Potter and the Philosopher's Stone* was published, the foreign rights for the book were up for auction at a book fair in Bologna, Italy. Christopher Little called to tell Rowling that American publishers were bidding on her book. He said that the bidding had reached $10,000 for the U.S. publishing rights. "They were up to five figures," Rowling recalls. "I went cold with shock."[81]

Little did Rowling know that the bidding had just begun. Arthur A. Levine, an editorial director at Scholastic, was prepared to go much higher than $10,000. He had read the book on his plane ride from New York to Bologna. "The thing I loved the most about reading Harry Potter is the idea of growing up unappreciated, feeling outcast and then this great satisfaction of being discovered," Levine later wrote. "That is the fantasy of every person who grows up feeling marginalized in any way. Along with the imagination and the wonderful writing, that's the emotional connection that drew me to the book."[82] Levine

Whose Stone?

J.K. Rowling called her first book *Harry Potter and the Philosopher's Stone*. The title refers to the legendary stone thought to be capable of turning base metals such as lead into gold and restoring youth to the aged. The executives at Scholastic who purchased the American rights to the book did not believe American children were familiar with the term and thought they would be turned off by the word "philosopher." Focusing on the stone's magical properties, the Scholastic executives suggested that "sorcerer" replace "philosopher" in the title.

Rowling opposed the effort to rename her book. Not being an expert on American culture, however, she eventually gave in. The book appeared in the United States as *Harry Potter and the Sorcerer's Stone*, and throughout the novel the characters refer to the magic stone by its newfangled name.

For those who simply enjoy an exciting story, the difference is not important; but for those whose reading experience is deepened and enriched by Rowling's artful brew of historical, mythological, and literary references, the absence of the philosopher's stone from the American edition takes a bit of the luster off of the book.

decided that the book had all the qualities of a classic, and he would treat it as such.

As the bidding climbed toward the $50,000 mark, however, Levine began to wonder if he should drop out. "It's a scary thing when you keep bidding and the stakes get higher and higher," he remembers. "It's one thing to say I love this first novel by this unknown woman in Scotland and I want to publish it. And it's another thing as the bidding goes higher. Do you love it this much? Do you love it at $50,000? At $70,000?"[83]

Levine decided he did. One bidder offered $100,000 for the rights, but Levine would not back down. He bid $105,000. It was enough. "I had never paid so much for an acquisition before,"[84] Levine recalls.

When the bidding was over, Levine called Rowling. She was stunned to hear the price he had paid for her work. "My reaction was shock," Rowling remembers. "This was like being catapulted into fairyland."[85]

Making Headlines

By bidding the largest sum ever paid to a first-time children's author, Levine drew more attention to Rowling than any public relations campaign could have. "A penniless and newly-divorced mother has sold her first book for £100,000,"[86] blared a headline in the *Daily Mail*, inadvertently reporting the selling price in pounds rather than dollars. Rowling's rags-to-riches story proved irresistible. The same weekend that Scholastic bought the U.S. rights, the *Sunday Times* ran a one thousand-word feature story on Rowling.

Bloomsbury made the most out of the media's interest in Rowling. The publisher arranged for an interview with Nigel Reynolds, the arts correspondent for the *Daily Telegraph*. "A young author has sold her first book to an American publisher for more than £100,000," Reynolds began, repeating the error in the *Daily Mail* headline. "What makes the deal remarkable is that Joanne Rowling's tome is not a novel or a heavyweight biography, but a children's story."[87]

Reynolds found Rowling to be "a little bit anxious" about all the attention she was getting. "I told her that if all goes well then she would find her life becoming public property," Reynolds remembers. "She seemed as though she was worried about that."[88]

Pressure

Reynolds did not know how right he was. Calm on the outside, Rowling was roiling on the inside. Rowling later told Geordie Greig of *Tatler* magazine:

I've never said this before, but when I was repeatedly asked, "How are you coping?" I would say, "Fine." I was lying to myself at the time. Denial was my friend. The truth is that I could easily have said, "Well, now you mention it, it's all quite difficult to deal with. I will go home this evening on my own to look after my daughter, and I will feel enormous pressure." I was isolated before I got famous, and having fame on top of an already isolating situation didn't help.

I was hypersensitive because I had a daughter from my first marriage. It was as though I'd lived under a rock for a long time and suddenly someone had lifted it off and was shining a torch onto me. And it's not that life under the rock was awful but actually I was petrified and didn't know how to handle it.[89]

Aware of the rising expectations about her work, Rowling began to worry that *Chamber of Secrets* was not as good as it could be. A week after handing in the manuscript, Rowling asked for it back. She kept it for six weeks. "I've only suffered writer's block badly once, and that was during the writing of *Chamber of Secrets*," she later confessed. "I had my first burst of publicity about the first book, and it paralyzed me. I was scared the second book wouldn't measure up, but I got through it!"[90] Satisfied at last with the second book, Rowling returned the manuscript to her publisher and began work on the third book of the series, *Harry Potter and the Prisoner of Azkaban*.

Accolades for the First Book

While the publicity nearly derailed Rowling's second book, it spurred sales of the first one. *Harry Potter and the Philosopher's Stone* landed on British best-seller lists in the summer of 1997 and stayed there throughout the year. By the end of its first year, the book had sold more than seventy thousand copies in the United Kingdom alone. Meanwhile, in the United States, Scholastic planned an initial print run of another fifty thousand copies.

Publicity was not the sole cause of the book's success, of course. The story itself was widely acclaimed. In November 1997 *Harry Potter and the Philosopher's Stone* received the Smarties Prize, one of Britain's most prestigious awards for children's literature. It also claimed the Federation of Children's Book Groups Award and was named the British Book Awards Children's Book of the Year.

While promoting her best-selling books, the enormously successful J.K. Rowling waves to hundreds of fans in London in 2000.

Rowling began to enjoy the comfort and security that her new career was bringing her. She moved into an apartment with a sitting room, a kitchen, two bedrooms, and a converted attic space. For the first time, Jessica had a bedroom of her own and Rowling had an office. Still, Rowling watched her budget closely. She explains, "If you have been through three or four years of worrying on a daily basis about the money running out, you are never going to forget what that's like."[91]

Harry Conquers America

Rowling had little to fear. When *Harry Potter and the Chamber of Secrets* was released in July 1998, it debuted as the top-selling book in the United Kingdom. A month later, Scholastic released *Harry Potter and the Philosopher's Stone*, which it renamed *Harry*

A display at a New York City bookstore in 1999 features the first three books in the Harry Potter series.

Potter and the Sorcerer's Stone, in the United States. The book flew to the top of *Publishers Weekly's* list of best-selling children's fiction. By mid-December online retailer Amazon.com reported that *Sorcerer's Stone* was its second-best-selling book. To satisfy demand, Scholastic went back to press seven times. By the end of December, more than 190,000 copies were in print in the United States.

Newsweek noted the book's success. "A dark British kids' book bewitches U.S.," ran the magazine's headline. Reporters Carla Power and Shehnaz Suterwalla wrote, "As melancholy as it is fantastic, 'Harry Potter' has been likened to the dark juvenile novels of Roald Dahl and C. S. Lewis." Noting the success of the book's sequel in the United Kingdom, the reporters declared, "It's clear that the author is no one-shot wonder."[92]

They were right. As soon as American fans heard that a sequel to *Harry Potter and the Sorcerer's Stone* was available in the UK, they began to order it online from Bloomsbury. Scholastic had planned to release *Harry Potter and the Chamber of Secrets* in September, but seeing orders slipping away to the British publisher, Scholastic rushed the book into print. Meanwhile, *Time* magazine fed the growing frenzy with an article that praised Rowling for conjuring up "a magical, self-contained parallel universe" that is "filled not only with characters familiar to most kids but also with clever jokes about garden gnomes and wizard chess—played with living pieces." Reporter Elizabeth Gleick concluded, "The *Wizard of Oz* just may have to make a little space on the shelf for the wizards of Hogwarts."[93]

Global Phenomenon

Scholastic issued *Harry Potter and the Chamber of Secrets* in June 1999. By July more than 900,000 copies were in print in the United States. More than 860,000 copies of *Harry Potter and the Sorcerer's Stone* also were in print. Both books landed on the *New York Times* best-seller list. The series was translated into twenty-five languages and was sold in 115 countries. Five million copies of the books were in print worldwide. Rowling's royalty checks, which were paid every six months, began to reflect the boom in sales. That summer, Rowling received a royalty check for £1 million ($1.5 million).

On Thursday, July 8, 1999, Bloomsbury released the third book in the series, *Harry Potter and the Prisoner of Azkaban*. Bookstores were instructed not to start selling copies until 3:45 P.M., the time when British schools let out. Tara Stephenson, the head of sales at Blackwell's Children's Bookshop in Oxford, said that once the witching hour had arrived, "There was a pause, then once the first one was sold, it was an absolute tidal wave."[94] By 4:15 P.M., Blackwell's had sold ninety-two copies of the new book. The scene was repeated throughout the United Kingdom. Within two weeks, the book had gone through ten printings and had sold in excess of 270,000 copies.

Plot Complications

After a brief tour of the United States, Rowling settled in to complete the fourth book of her seven-book series. It turned out to be the most difficult of the books to write. For one thing, it was much longer than the first three books. "I knew from the beginning it would be the biggest of the first four," Rowling later said. "It's a complex plot, and you don't rush a plot that complex, because everyone's gonna get confused."[95]

As it turned out, even the author herself got confused. "I should have put that plot under a microscope," Rowling told *Entertainment Weekly*. "I wrote what I thought was half the book, and 'Ack!' Huge gaping hole in the middle of the plot."[96] Since Rowling's plots and subplots are tightly entwined, she found that she had to unbraid and reweave nearly half of the book. Rowling wrote for ten hours a day to get the book back on schedule. Despite the effort, Rowling missed her deadline by two months.

Harry the Fourth

After finishing the book, Rowling met with the press, but she refused to divulge the title of her new work. Critics said her silence was a strategy designed to build interest in the book.

Rowling disputed the charge. "It wasn't even a marketing ploy," she says. "It came from me. This book was the culmination of ten years' work, and something very big in terms of my ongoing plot happens at the end. Had that got out, there's no way the book would have been as enjoyable to read."[97]

Girl Guide Rowling

As a youth, J.K. Rowling belonged to Girlguiding U.K., part of the World Association of Girl Guides and Gift Scouts. A former Brownie and Guide, Rowling was interviewed as part of a campaign by Girlguiding Scotland to inspire young women with examples of talented women from Scotland:

How would you describe Scotland to someone who had never been?

It is one of the most hauntingly beautiful places in the world, the history is fascinating, the men are handsome and the whisky is delicious. But don't eat the macaroni pies.

Do you think Hermione has the right skills and attributes to become a good Guide?

I can easily imagine Hermione in the Guides, given that she's resourceful, highly motivated and eager to learn. She might be a little over-competitive when it came to interest badges, though.

What is the greatest gift your mother gave you?

She was the one who read to us when we were little, filled the house with books, loved discussing her favourite novels and never sat down without something to read, so I would have to say a love of literature. However, she also taught me how to make a decent Yorkshire pudding.

Quoted in Carrie Blake, "Inspirational Women," Girlguiding Scotland, April 2006. www.girl guidingscotland.org.uk/information/info_interview_rowling.htm.

The Harry Potter phenomenon achieves a distinctive mark of success by being the subject of a Time magazine cover in 1999.

To preserve the secret, no advance copies were given to reviewers or members of the press. The printers shipped the books in boxes marked "HARRY POTTER IV, NOT TO BE SOLD BEFORE JULY 8, 2000."[98] Worried that someone might raid the Bloomsbury offices to get a peek at the book, Rowling's editor locked the manuscript in a bank vault. Despite the precautions, the cover jacket and the title, *Harry Potter and the Goblet of Fire*, leaked out on June 26. A few days later a clerk at a Wal-Mart in Virginia sold a copy of the book to eight-year-old Laura Cantwell of Fairfax, who shared her lucky find with the media.

The leaks did not spoil the book's debut. Thousands of children lined up at bookstores in Britain, Canada, and the United States to buy the first copies. Some bookstores stayed open past midnight so fans could buy the book at 12:01 A.M. on July 8. Enterprising booksellers such as Steve Moore of Toronto dressed up as wizards and hosted pajama parties to celebrate the midnight event. The Tattered Cover Bookstore in Denver, Colorado, served late-night patrons a brew of ginger ale and apple juice to mimic Harry Potter's favorite beverage, butter beer. One thousand people showed up at Vancouver's Kidsbooks for a publication party at 11 P.M., but co-owners Phyllis Simon and Kelly McKinnon had to turn half the crowd away. "Five hundred is all the fire regulations would allow,"[99] explained Simon.

Online retailer Amazon.com teamed up with Federal Express to deliver 250,000 copies of the book on the first day at no extra charge to their customers. Amazon reported that it logged 325,000 preorders in the weeks leading up to the publication— eight times more than its previous high. Scholastic ordered the largest first printing in history, 3.8 million copies for the United States alone. Bloomsbury also ordered the largest print run in its history. Rowling earned $10 million in royalties just from the first printings.

Chapter Five

Happy Endings

Three weeks after the release of *Harry Potter and the Goblet of Fire*, J.K. Rowling celebrated her thirty-fifth birthday. She already had accomplished more than she ever thought possible. She had a beautiful daughter. She had published four best-selling books. She had accumulated wealth beyond her wildest dreams. Yet at times she felt "very lonely." She had always imagined that, like her parents had, she would find a companion for life. As her fame and wealth grew, however, she began to doubt that would happen. She feared that men would be attracted to her because of her station in life, and not for who she was. "I had thought . . . that [wealth] would be a factor in my staying single forever," she recalls. "I thought, 'I'm not going to meet anyone.' I did believe that. I cannot emphasize that enough."[100]

Despite her loneliness, Rowling did not feel sorry for herself. She was proud of the life she had made for herself and her daughter. "I thought, 'I've been lucky. I've got my work. I had my child.' I couldn't complain," she remembers. "I am a coper. I can do the being-on-my-own thing."[101]

With her financial fortune growing, Rowling bought a home in London so she could be closer to her publisher and the center of British culture. Purchased for £4.5 million ($6.75 million), the mansion has an underground swimming pool and twenty-four-hour security. Rowling also bought a country home known as Killiechassie House, near Aberfeldy, Scotland.

Giving Back

Vast wealth did not change the young woman who grew up admiring Jessica Mitford. Rowling felt an ever greater responsibility for helping others, in part because her money made her uncomfortable. "I feel guilty," she told Jeremy Paxman of the BBC. "The rewards were disproportionate."[102] Rowling resolved to share her success with worthy causes. Remembering the difficulties she had faced as a single mother, she donated £500,000 ($925,000) to the National Council for One Parent Families.

Rowling was not satisfied, however. As in her days at Amnesty International, she wanted to reach beyond the borders of her own country to help children in need. She teamed up

The unprecedented success of the Harry Potter series allowed J.K. Rowling to buy this stately home in the Scottish highlands near Aberfeldy.

with Comic Relief U.K., a charity that uses humorous campaigns to raise money for the needy. Instead of simply writing a check to the organization, Rowling used her pen to draft two new books, *Quidditch Through the Ages* and *Fantastic Beasts and Where to Find Them*, with the understanding that proceeds from their sale would go to Comic Relief. Worldwide sales of Rowling's two books raised more than £6 million ($11.1 million) for the organization.

"The Most Meaningful Thing"

More than anything, Rowling wanted to help those stricken with the disease that took her mother's life. In 2001 Rowling became a patron of the MS Society Scotland, donating money to the organization, giving speeches on its behalf, and writing articles to raise awareness about MS. In 2002 she hosted a Halloween ball at Stirling Castle to raise money for the organiza-

On a 2006 visit to Romania to champion children's welfare, Rowling poses with children in foster care in Bucharest.

tion. When the receipts were counted, the society had raised £275,000 ($509,000).

One month later Rowling teamed with the MS Society again to help find a cure for the disease. The MS Society Scotland gave a £500,000 ($925,000) grant—largely funded by Rowling—to the University of Aberdeen to create a special research group. "I'm proud to be supporting this vital research fellowship through which some of the best experts in the field are joining forces to strike back at MS,"[103] Rowling said.

On March 17, 2006, Rowling hosted another fundraising event at Stirling Castle: the Masquerade for MS Ball. The 250 masked guests enjoyed a lavish banquet, live music, and a treasure hunt for a bejeweled silver mask. Rowling herself wrote the clues for the treasure hunt. Proceeds from the event totaled more than £250,000 ($463,000). "For me, being able to campaign and fund-raise for multiple sclerosis is the most personally meaningful thing to have come out of being famous," Rowling says. "It would mean everything to me if I thought even one person did not have to go through what my mother did."[104]

A month later, the MS Society Scotland announced that it was giving a £2.1 million ($3.9 million) grant to Edinburgh University's Centre for Regenerative Medicine to help search for a cure for MS. A substantial portion of the grant came from Rowling.

Magical Meeting

While Rowling was working on her fund-raising books for Comic Relief in late 2000, she attended a dinner party given by one of her friends. One of the guests was a young doctor named Neil Murray. Rowling and Murray felt an instant attraction to one another. To Rowling's relief, Murray seemed unfazed by her wealth and fame. "Money just wasn't an issue with him," she recalls. "In fact, Neil doesn't really spend money. That's not what he wants."[105]

What Murray wanted was to spend time with Rowling. The two dated, attended events together, traveled together, and fell in love. While vacationing on Mauritius, an island in the Indian Ocean, Rowling and Murray were photographed on the beach.

A British newspaper published the pictures, speculating that Rowling and Murray had secretly married. In a letter to the *Scotsman* newspaper, Rowling smothered the rumor with sarcasm: "Some people seem to need reminding that wearing a swimsuit in the vicinity of a man in shorts does not constitute a marriage ceremony, even in Mauritius."[106]

The truth was that marriage was becoming a possibility for the single author. "Certainly before I met Neil I hadn't met anyone that I could conceive of marrying," Rowling later said. "I'm not someone who will take just anyone."[107] Murray was not just anyone, however. Handsome and easygoing with a good sense of humor, the doctor was the perfect match for Rowling. When he proposed marriage, Rowling accepted. They married in a private ceremony on Boxing Day, December 26, 2001.

A Growing Family

The newlyweds were eager to have children, and in September 2002 they announced that they were expecting a baby. Rowling was in the middle of writing the fifth Harry Potter book, *Harry Potter and the Order of the Phoenix*. Knowing that caring for a newborn would consume large amounts of time, Rowling raced to finish the book before the baby arrived. She told Paxman that at times she felt so much pressure to get the book done that she considered breaking her arm so she would have an excuse not to write. On January 15, 2003, Rowling announced that the book—the longest in the series to that point—was complete. Two months later, on March 25, Rowling gave birth to her second child, a boy the couple named David Gordon Rowling Murray.

When the long-awaited *Harry Potter and the Order of the Phoenix* was released on June 21, 2003, hundreds of bookstores worldwide were open at midnight so fans could buy the book as soon as it was available. At Waterstone's West End bookshop in Edinburgh, more than three hundred patrons—many dressed as witches and wizards—lined up outside awaiting the book's release. Inside was a surprise: J.K. Rowling sat at a table waiting to autograph copies of the new book. She recalls, "When *Goblet of Fire* was published I was desperate to

Rowling and her husband, Neil Murray, attend an event in Scotland in 2006.

go into a bookshop at midnight and see children's reactions, so this time I'm really pleased I could. Much of the pleasure of being published for me is meeting the children who are reading the books."[108]

Harry Potter and the Order of the Phoenix shattered all records set by its predecessors. Sales of *Order of the Phoenix* helped make Rowling the first author in history to attain a net worth of $1 billion. Not all of that money came from the sale of her books, however. A large portion came from royalties from a series of motion pictures based on the books.

Harry Goes to Hollywood

Less than a month after *Harry Potter and the Philosopher's Stone* was released, four film companies offered Rowling contracts for the movie rights to her novel. Rowling was delighted by the idea of seeing her characters come to life on the big screen, but she was not in a rush to proceed. She and Christopher Little wanted to establish the book series as a success so they could control what kind of film would be made. Their strategy paid off. After the success of the first three books, Rowling and Little were able to make a motion picture deal that met all of their financial and artistic requirements.

Rowling insisted from the start that any movie made from her books would have to be live action, not animated. No new characters would be introduced and none could be eliminated. The U.S. motion picture company Warner Bros. agreed to these terms, and in late 1999 Rowling signed a deal with the studio for about $1 million.

Warner Bros. chose Chris Columbus, director of box-office hits *Home Alone*, *Mrs. Doubtfire*, and *Gremlins*, to direct the first movie. "It was important to us to find a director who has an affinity for both children and magic,"[109] says Lorenzo di Bonaventura, Warner Bros.' president of worldwide theatrical production.

The task of adapting the book to a screenplay was given to Steve Kloves, a nineteen-year Hollywood veteran. Kloves believed the success of the movie depended on bringing Rowling's characters to life. "Obviously you need a plot, but the charm of

Rowling Reaches Out to a Fan

Nine-year-old Catie Hoch of Albany, New York, was a huge Harry Potter fan. Like other children her age, Catie loved to escape into the world of wizards and witches that J.K. Rowling had created. Catie had more to escape from than most kids did, however. At the age of five, Catie had been diagnosed with neuroblastoma, a type of cancer. The disease spread from her kidney to her liver, lungs, and spinal column. Catie fought the disease, but suffered a relapse. In 2000 doctors informed her mother, Gina Peca, that Catie had only weeks to live.

Trying to find ways to make Catie's last days as happy as possible, Peca wrote to Rowling's publishers, asking about the then-unpublished fourth book in the Harry Potter series. To Peca's amazement, she received an e-mail from Rowling herself. Catie wrote back, and the author and her fan began to exchange e-mails and gifts. When Rowling learned that Catie had only a few days to live, she called the hospital and spoke with Catie. Rowling delighted the youngster by reading chapters from *Harry Potter and the Goblet of Fire* over the phone.

A few days later, Catie died. Peca and Catie's father, Larry Hoch, set up a foundation in Catie's name to help fund research into neuroblastoma. In its first two years the charity raised a total of £69,000 ($127,725). In December 2002 the foundation received a check for £57,000 ($105,512), nearly doubling what the foundation had raised. The check was a gift from J.K. Rowling.

the movie should be these kids, and you have to be as faithful as possible,"[110] he said.

A Spell of Casting

If Kloves was right about the importance of the characters, then the casting of the actors to play those roles would be crucial. Rowling suggested that the burly Scottish actor Robbie Coltrane would be perfect for the part of Hagrid, the Hogwarts groundskeeper.

Irish film star Richard Harris, who had played King Arthur in the 1967 musical *Camelot* signed on to play Dumbledore. Two-time Academy Award-winning actress Dame Maggie Smith was cast as Professor McGonagall. John Cleese, a veteran of the comedy troupe Monty Python, played Nearly Headless Nick, a ghost that haunts the Hogwarts dining hall.

Worried that recognizable faces would ruin the movie's believability, Warner Bros. looked for unknown actors to play the roles of Harry Potter, Hermione Granger, and Ron Weasley. Ten-year-old Emma Watson won the part of Hermione, and eleven-year-old Rupert Grint was cast as Ron. More than sixty thousand boys auditioned for the part of Harry Potter, but none seemed quite right. Everyone, including Rowling, joined in the hunt for the hero. One evening Warner Bros. executive David Heyman went to a play with his friend Alan Radcliffe, who brought along his eleven-year-old son, Daniel. "I was watching the play but the details melted into the background after I saw Dan," Heyman recalls. "I thought Dan so clearly embodied the spirit of Harry."[111] Columbus and Rowling agreed, and Radcliffe got the part.

In London Rowling poses with (left to right) Rupert Grint, Daniel Radcliffe, and Emma Watson at the premiere of Harry Potter and the Philosopher's Stone *in 2001.*

The marquee of the Odeon Theater in London advertises the world premiere of Harry Potter and the Philosopher's Stone *in November 2001.*

World Premiere

The premiere was held at the Odeon Theater in Leicester Square, London, on November 4, 2001. Set designers decorated the front of the theater to look like Hogwarts School. About five thousand fans—many in costume—showed up to get a glimpse of Rowling and other celebrities. Taking in the hysteria that greeted her arrival, Rowling remarked, "This is not what you think about when you write a book." Afterward Rowling said she was "happy and relieved"[112] that the film remained faithful to the book.

Not everyone was enchanted. "The most highly awaited movie of the year has a dreary, literal-minded competence, following the letter of the law as laid down by the author," wrote Elvis Mitchell of the *New York Times*. "A lack of imagination pervades the movie because it so slavishly follows the book."[113]

However, most Harry Potter fans did not share the critics' view. "The movie skipped part of the book, but I thought it was great,"[114] said ten-year-old Jeffrey Chyau of New York.

Box-Office Magic

Studio executives expected a large turnout for the movie, but few expected the film to set records. Nevertheless *Harry Potter and the Sorcerer's Stone* broke the single-day record for movie receipts in the United States, raking in $31.6 million. The movie became the top-grossing film of the year in the United States, earning more than $286 million in just two months.

The cast and director reunited to make the second movie of the series, *Harry Potter and the Chamber of Secrets*. Released on November 15, 2003, the second installment broke box-office records in the UK, becoming the first film to gross £10 million ($18.5 million) in its opening weekend. By the time its theatrical release was complete, *Chamber of Secrets* had earned $866.3 million worldwide, compared to $966.6 million worldwide for *Sorcerer's Stone*.

Change of Direction

For the third movie in the series, *Harry Potter and the Prisoner of Azkaban*, Warner Bros. hired a new director, Alfonso Cuarón. Born in Mexico City, Cuarón had directed several films, including the popular coming-of-age movie *Y Tu Mamá También* (*And Your Mother, Too*).

Cuarón's vision of Rowling's work was darker and more ominous than his predecessor's, in part because the characters were older and faced more dangerous situations. Cuarón made changes to the story, the costuming, and the characters. The most obvious departure from the book was the introduction of a talking

Alfonso Cuarón, director of **Harry Potter and the Prisoner of Azkaban,** *stands in front of a movie poster.*

shrunken head to the Knight Bus that Harry Potter boards at the beginning of *Harry Potter and the Prisoner of Azkaban.* Although Rowling generally resists changes to the enchanted world she has created, she did not object to Cuarón's invention. "I thought the shrunken head was very funny, I really liked that," she remarks. "I said to Steve Kloves many a time, 'I wish I had written that.'"[115]

Released on 7,804 screens in twenty-four countries on June 4, 2004, *Harry Potter and the Prisoner of Azkaban* broke the box-office record for a worldwide motion picture release, taking in $114 million on its opening weekend. In the end, *Harry Potter and the Prisoner of Azkaban* earned $789.5 million worldwide—less than the previous Harry Potter films, but still a hit.

Four's a Charm

Like other popular movie series, such as the *Star Wars* series, the Harry Potter movies continued to build their fan base from year to year. The growing size of the Harry Potter audience and rising ticket prices combined to help the next movie in the series, *Harry Potter and the Goblet of Fire*, surpass the opening weekends of its predecessors. Opening on November 18, 2005, *Harry Potter and the Goblet of Fire* grossed $102.3 million in its debut weekend in the United States alone. The film went on to earn more than $892 million worldwide, making it the second-highest-grossing Harry Potter film.

Warner Bros. picked English director Mike Newell to guide the making of the fourth Harry Potter film. Three actors joined the regular Harry Potter cast: Miranda Richardson as Rita Skeeter,

Portrait of the Artist as a "Ruthless Killer"

In an interview with Jeremy Paxman, J.K. Rowling discussed the emotional toll her writing sometimes takes on her. She described a discussion she had with her husband, Dr. Neil Murray, after she had written an episode in which one of her characters died:

> I had re-written the death, re-written it and that was it. And the person was definitely dead. . . . And I walked into the kitchen crying and Neil said to me, "What on Earth is wrong?" and I said, "I've just killed the person." Neil doesn't know who the person is. And he said, "Well, don't do it then.". . . I said, "It just doesn't work like that." You are writing children's books, you need to be a ruthless killer.

Quoted in "Tears of a 'Ruthless Killer,' but Definitely No Writer's Block," *Scotsman*, June 18, 2003. http://news.scotsman.com/topics.cfm?tid=3&id=670572003.

Brendan Gleeson as Mad-Eye Moody, and Ralph Fiennes as Lord Voldemort. More violent than the first three Harry Potter films, *Harry Potter and the Goblet of Fire* showed Harry in another life-or-death struggle with evil. "Childhood ends for Harry Potter, the young wizard with the zigzag scar and phantasmagorical world of troubles, not long after the dragons have roared and the mer-people have screeched their empty threats through broken teeth,"[116] wrote *New York Times* film critic Manohla Dargis.

The violence of the movie reflected Rowling's own artistic vision. "If you are writing about Good and Evil, there comes a point where you have to get serious," she told Roxanne Feldman of *School Library Journal*:

> Early on, I had to consider how to depict an evil being, such as Lord Voldemort. . . . I could go one of two ways: I could either make him a pantomime villain . . . [meaning that there is] a lot of sound and thunder and nobody really gets hurt. Or [I could] attempt to do something a little bit more serious—which means you're going to have to show death. And worse than that, you'll have to show the death of characters whom the readers care about. I chose the second route.[117]

More Good News

Although Rowling consulted with the directors throughout the filming of the Harry Potter movies, she did not stop working on her books. Throughout 2003 and most of 2004, Rowling worked on the sixth book of the series. During that time she became pregnant with her third child. On her official Web site, Rowling joked about the pregnancy. "The distance between the keyboard and yours truly increases day by day as my third child races Harry's next adventure into the world," she wrote. "I will soon need extendable fingers to type."[118] Rowling completed the manuscript on December 21, 2004, four days ahead of schedule, and announced the title of the new work: *Harry Potter and the Half-Blood Prince*.

A month later, on January 23, 2005, Rowling gave birth to her third child—another girl. "Neil and I are absolutely delighted to say that our new daughter arrived on Sunday evening," Rowling wrote on her Web site two days later. "Her name is Mackenzie Murray (middle names Jean Rowling) and she is ridiculously beautiful, though I suppose I might be biased."[119]

Rowling took a short break from writing to care for her infant daughter. In the meantime, her publisher prepared for the release of *Harry Potter and the Half-Blood Prince*. According to Scholastic, 6.9 million American readers got their first look at the new book within the first twenty-four hours the book was on sale, breaking the one-day sales record set by *Harry Potter and the Order of the Phoenix*. The book was a critical success as well, taking the prestigious Book of the Year award at the British Book Awards in 2006.

The End

As Rowling turned forty in the summer of 2005, one goal remained: to complete the seven-part story she had begun fifteen years earlier. Rowling sensed that ending the series would take an emotional toll on her. On Christmas Day 2005, Rowling left her fans a gift-wrapped message on the virtual desktop of her Web site:

> 2006 will be the year when I write the final book in the Harry Potter series. I contemplate the task with mingled feelings of excitement and dread, because I can't wait to get started, to tell the final part of the story and, at last, to answer all the questions (will I ever answer all of the questions? Let's aim for most of the questions); and yet it will all be over at last and I can't quite imagine life without Harry.

> However (clears throat in stern British manner) this is no time to get maudlin.[120]

At the British Book Awards three months later, Rowling paused to speak with a reporter who asked how the new book was coming. "It's going very well," Rowling said. "I've done a bit. But there's nothing more I can tell you. Everything's a giveaway now."[121]

Rowling has been vague about what she will do after the series is finished. She told Geordie Greig that she had already written a new children's book for readers younger than the Harry

J.K. Rowling, active in charity work, addresses a press conference in 2006 before participating in a fundraiser with other authors.

Potter audience. Rowling described the unnamed book as a "political fairy story" about a monster. "I haven't even told my publisher about this,"[122] Rowling confessed.

Some observers doubt that Rowling will be able to write anything that approaches the success of Harry Potter. While she may never again be struck with a lightning bolt of inspiration like the one she experienced on the train between Manchester and London in 1990, by the time she finishes the series she will have more than a decade of experience as a novelist to draw on for her next work.

Rowling has said that the final chapter of the final book is already written. It lies in a safe, waiting to be joined to the narrative that hurtles toward it. The last word of the last book is "scar."[123] Even if Rowling never writes another word after that, she already has achieved immortality as the creator of the orphan boy who learned he was a wizard just in time to take up his wand against the dark forces that threaten the world.

Introduction: The Return of the Written Word

1. Quoted in Arthur MacMillan, "Potter Works Wonders for Kids' Literacy," *Scotland on Sunday*, July 10, 2005. http://news.scotsman.com/scotland.cfm?id=765922005.
2. Paul Gray, "The Magic of Potter," *Time*, December 25, 2000–January 1, 2001, p. 116.
3. Quoted in Gray, "The Magic of Potter," p. 118.

Chapter 1: Growing Imagination

4. J.K. Rowling, *The Not Especially Fascinating Life So Far of J.K. Rowling*. www.cliphoto.com/potter/rowling.htm.
5. Sean Smith, *J.K. Rowling: A Biography*. London: Michael O'Mara Books, 2001, p. 13.
6. Quoted in Lindsey Fraser, *Conversations with J.K. Rowling*. New York: Scholastic, 2000, p. 11.
7. Quoted in Matt Seaton, "If I Could Talk to My Mum Again I'd Tell Her I Had a Daughter—and I Wrote Some Books and Guess What Happened?" *Guardian Unlimited* (Manchester), April 18, 2001. http://books.guardian.co.uk/harrypotternews/0,,541346.00.html.
8. Quoted in Helena de Bertodano, "Harry Potter Charms a Nation," *Telegraph* (London), July 25, 1998. www.quick-quote-quill.org/articles/1998/0798-telegraph-bertodano.html.
9. Rowling, *The Not Especially Fascinating Life So Far of J.K. Rowling*.
10. Quoted in Helen M. Jerome and Jerome V. Kramer, "Author's Childhood Friend Says He Was Inspiration for Harry Potter," *Book*, March/April 2000. www.bookmagazine.com/archive/issue9/potter.shtml.
11. Rowling, *The Not Especially Fascinating Life So Far of J.K. Rowling*.
12. Rowling, *The Not Especially Fascinating Life So Far of J.K. Rowling*.

13. Amazon.co.uk, "J.K. Rowling's Interview with Amazon.co.uk." www.cliphoto.com/potter/interview.htm.
14. Quoted in Roxanne Feldman, "The Truth About Harry," *School Library Journal*, September 1, 1999. www.school libraryjournal.com/article/CA153024.html.
15. Quoted in de Bertodano, "Harry Potter Charms a Nation."
16. Rowling, *The Not Especially Fascinating Life So Far of J.K. Rowling.*
17. Quoted in Geordie Greig, "Special JK," *Tatler*, February 2006, p. 130.
18. J.K. Rowling, *Harry Potter and the Chamber of Secrets*. New York: Scholastic, 1999, p. v.
19. Rowling, *The Not Especially Fascinating Life So Far of J.K. Rowling.*
20. Quoted in Malcolm Jones, "The Return of Harry Potter!" *Newsweek*, July 10, 2000, p. 60.

Chapter 2: "It Was Like Research"

21. Quoted in Fraser, *Conversations with J.K. Rowling*, p. 38.
22. Quoted in Malcolm Jones, "Magician for Millions," *Newsweek*, August 23, 1999, p. 59.
23. Quoted in Jones, "The Return of Harry Potter!" p. 60.
24. Quoted in Jones, "The Return of Harry Potter!" p. 60.
25. Quoted in Jones, "The Return of Harry Potter!" p. 58.
26. Quoted in Fraser, *Conversations with J.K. Rowling*, p. 38.
27. Quoted in Scholastic.com, "Transcript of J.K. Rowling's Live Interview," February 3, 2000. www.scholastic.com/harry potter/author/transcript1.htm.
28. Quoted in Teachervision.com, "Lesson Plans: Questions and Answers with J.K. Rowling." www.teachervision.com/lesson-plans/lesson-2693.html.
29. Quoted in Fraser, *Conversations with J.K. Rowling*, pp. 26–27.
30. Quoted in Fraser, *Conversations with J.K. Rowling*, p. 39.
31. Quoted in Harry Potter Galleries, "Barnesandnoble.com Chat Transcript," March 19, 1999. http://history.250x.com/vaults/c105.htm.
32. Maureen Dowd, "Veni, Vidi, Voldemort," *New York Times*, December 9, 2001, p. 4.13.

33. Quoted in Fraser, *Conversations with J.K. Rowling*, p. 31.
34. Quoted in Fraser, *Conversations with J.K. Rowling*, pp. 40–41.
35. Quoted in Fraser, *Conversations with J.K. Rowling*, p. 20.
36. Quoted in Fraser, *Conversations with J.K. Rowling*, p. 17.
37. Quoted in Margaret Weir, "Of Magic and Single Motherhood," Salon.com, March 31, 1999. www.salon.com/mwt/feature/1999/03/cov_31featureb.html.
38. Quoted in Harry Potter Galleries, "Chat Transcript."
39. Quoted in Linda Richards, "January Profile: J.K. Rowling." *January Magazine*, October 2000. www.januarymagazine.com/profiles/jkrowling.html.
40. Quoted in Nancy Gibbs, "Harry Is an Old Soul," *Time*, December 25, 2000–January 1, 2001, p. 119.
41. Quoted in Scholastic.com, "Transcript of J.K. Rowling's Live Interview," www.scholastic.com/harrypotter/author/transcript2.htm.
42. Quoted in Anne Johnstone, "Happy Ending, and That's for Beginners." *Herald* (Glasgow, Scotland), June 24, 1997, p. 14.
43. Quoted in Seaton, "If I Could Talk to My Mum Again."
44. Quoted in Greig, "Special JK," p. 130.
45. Quoted in Greig, "Special JK," p. 130.
46. Quoted in Greig, "Special JK," p. 130.
47. Quoted in Elizabeth Dunn, "From the Dole to Hollywood," *Telegraph* (London), August 2, 1997. www.quick-quote-quill.org/articles/1997/0897-telegraph-dunn.html.
48. Quoted in Greig, "Special JK," p. 130.
49. Quoted in Greig, "Special JK," p. 134.

Chapter 3: The Magic of Motherhood

50. Quoted in Fraser, *Conversations with J.K. Rowling*, p. 41.
51. Quoted in Smith, *J.K. Rowling*, p. 101.
52. Quoted in Smith, *J.K. Rowling*, p. 106.
53. Quoted in Smith, *J.K. Rowling*, p. 111.
54. Quoted in Smith, *J.K. Rowling*, p. 108.
54. Quoted in Smith, *J.K. Rowling*, p. 115.
56. Quoted in Seaton, "If I Could Talk to My Mum Again."
57. Quoted in Smith, *J.K. Rowling*, p. 121.

58. Quoted in Simon Hattenstone, "Harry, Jessie, and Me," *Guardian Unlimited* (Manchester), July 8, 2000. http://books.guardian.co.uk/print/0,,4037903-103425,00.html.
59. Quoted in David Robinson, "The Bullet-Proof Barrier Between City's Rich and Poor," *Scotsman* (Edinburgh), December 3, 2005. http://news.scotsman.com/topics.cfm?tid=3&id=2343542005.
60. Quoted in Hattenstone, "Harry, Jessie, and Me."
61. Quoted in Dunn, "From the Dole to Hollywood."
62. Quoted in Weir, "Of Magic and Single Motherhood."
63. Quoted in William Plummer and Joanna Blonska, "Spell Binder," *People*, July 12, 1999, p. 86.
64. Quoted in Jones, "Magician for Millions," p. 59.
65. Quoted in Seaton, "If I Could Talk to My Mum Again."
66. Quoted in Fraser, *Conversations with J.K. Rowling*, p. 44.
67. Quoted in Eddie Gibb, "Tales from a Single Mother," *Times* (London), June 29, 1997, p. 3.
68. Quoted in Smith, *J.K. Rowling*, p. 131.
69. Quoted in Anjana Ahuja, "Harry Potter's Novel Encounter," *Times* (London), June 27, 2000, p. 2.
70. Quoted in Smith, *J.K. Rowling*, p. 131.
71. Quoted in Nigel Reynolds, "£100,000 Success Story for Penniless Mother," *Telegraph* (London), July 7, 1997, p. 3.
72. Quoted in Ahuja, "Harry Potter's Novel Encounter," p. 208.
73. Quoted in Smith, *J.K. Rowling*, p. 136.
74. Quoted in Weir, "Of Magic and Single Motherhood."

Chapter 4: Miraculous Success
75. Quoted in Weir, "Of Magic and Single Motherhood."
76. Quoted in Hattenstone, "Harry, Jessie, and Me."
77. Quoted in Smith, *J.K. Rowling*, p. 160.
78. Quoted in Fraser, *Conversations with J.K. Rowling*, p. 46.
79. Quoted in Reynolds, "£100,000 Success Story," p. 3.
80. Nicolette Jones, "School's Out for Summer," *Times* (London), July 13 1997, Book Section, p. 9.
81. Quoted in Weir, "Of Magic and Single Motherhood."
82. Arthur A. Levine with Doreen Carvajal, "Why I Paid So Much," *New York Times*, October 13, 1999, p. C-16.

83. Levine with Carvajal, "Why I Paid So Much," p. C-16.
84. Levine with Carvajal, "Why I Paid So Much," p.C-16.
85. Quoted in Plummer and Blonska, "Spell Binder," p. 86.
86. Quoted in Smith, *J.K. Rowling*, p. 153.
87. Reynolds, "£100,000 Success Story," p. 3.
88. Quoted in Smith, *J.K. Rowling*, p. 155.
89. Quoted in Greig, "Special JK," p. 134.
90. Scholastic.com, "Transcript of J.K. Rowling's Live Interview," October 16, 2000. www.scholastic.com/harrypotter/author/transcript2.htm.
91. Quoted by Alan Cowell, "All Aboard the Harry Potter Promotional Express; An Author's Promotional Juggernaut Keeps Rolling On," *New York Times*, July 10, 2000, p. E-1.
92. Carla Power and Shehnaz Suterwalla, "A Literary Sorceress," *Newsweek*, December 7, 1998, p. 77.
93. Elizabeth Gleick, "The Wizard of Hogwarts," *Time*, April 12, 1999, p. 86.
94. Quoted in Elizabeth Gleick, "Abracadabra," *Time*, July 26, 1999, p. 72.
95. Quoted in Jeff Jenson, "'Fire' Storm," *Entertainment Weekly*, September 7, 2000, www.ew.com/ew/report/0,6115, 85523_5_00.html.
96. Quoted in Jenson, "'Fi re' Storm."
97. Quoted in Jenson, "'Fire' Storm."
98. Quoted in Malcolm Jones, "Why Harry's Hot," *Newsweek*, July 17, 2000, p. 54.
99. Quoted in Brian Bethune, "Harry Potter Inc.," *Maclean's*, July 17, 2000, p. 44.

Chapter 5: Happy Endings

100. Quoted in Greig, "Special JK," p. 134
101. Quoted in Greig, "Special JK," p. 134.
102. Quoted in Jane Hamilton, "JK Makes Rich List with $1 Bn Fortune," *Edinburgh Evening News*, February 26, 2004. http://news.scotsman.com/topics.cfm?tid=3&id=226402004.
103. Quoted in BBC News, "Rowling Backs MS Research," December 4, 2002. http://news.bbc.co.uk/1/hi/scotland/254 2143.stm.

104. Quoted in Rebecca McQuillan, "Rowling Finds Meaning in Fame," *Herald* (Glasgow), December 5, 2002, p. 14.
105. Quoted in Greig, "Special JK," p. 134.
106. Quoted in Auslan Cramb, "J K Rowling Denies Having Writer's Block over Next Harry Potter Book," *Telegraph* (London), August 8, 2001. www.portal.telegraph.co.uk/news/main.jhtml?xml=/news/2001/08/10/npot10.xml.
107. Quoted in Greig, "Special JK," p. 134.
108. Quoted in *Edinburgh Evening News*, "JK in City for Spell at Harry Launch," June 21, 2003. http://news.scotsman.com/topics.cfm?tid=3&id=682722003.
109. Quoted in Smith, *J.K. Rowling*, p. 176.
110. Quoted in Michael Sragow, "A Wizard of Hollywood," Salon.com, February 24, 2000. www.salon.com/ent/col/srag/2000/02/24/kloves/index3.html.
111. Quoted in Smith, *J.K. Rowling*, p. 179.
112. Quoted in BBC News, "Potter Casts Spell at World Première," November 5, 2001. http://news.bbc.co.uk/hi/entertainment/1634408.stm.
113. Elvis Mitchell, "Wizard School Without the Magic, *New York Times*, November 16, 2001. www.nytimes.com/2001/11/16/movies/16POTT.html.
114. Quoted in Seth Schiesel, "Young Viewers Like Screen Translation of 'Potter' Book," *New York Times*, November 19, 2001. www.nytimes.com/2001/11/19/movies/19 POTT. html.
115. J.K. Rowling, interview, *The Prisoner of Azkaban* DVD. Los Angeles, Warner Bros., 2004.
116. Manohla Dargis, "The Young Wizard Puts Away Childish Things," *New York Times*, November 17, 2005. http://movies2.nytimes.com/2005/11/17/movies/17pott.html.
117. Quoted in Feldman, "The Truth about Harry."
118. J.K. Rowling, "No News Is Good News," J.K. Rowling Official Site, December 10, 2004. www.jkrowling.com/en.
119. J.K. Rowling, "JKR Gives Birth to Baby Girl," J.K. Rowling Official Site, January 25, 2005. www.jkrowling.com/en.
120. Quoted in The Leaky Cauldron, "A Christmas Present from J.K. Rowling," December 24, 2005. www.the-leaky-cauldron.org/#article:8168.

121. Quoted in CBBC Newsround, "Half-Blood Prince Bags Book Prize," March 30, 2006. http://news.bbc.co.uk/cbbc news/hi/newsid_4850000/newsid_4859800/4859848.stm.

122. Quoted in Greig, "Special JK," p. 134.

123. "J.K. Rowling," *People*, December 31, 1999. p. 87.

Important Dates

1964

Anne Volant and Peter Rowling meet.

1965

Anne Volant and Peter Rowling marry; daughter Joanne, nicknamed Jo, born.

1967

Dianne Rowling, nicknamed Di, born.

1971

Jo writes down her first story; family moves to Winterbourne; Jo meets Ian and Vicki Potter.

1974

Family moves into Church Cottage in Tutshill; Jo enrolls at Tutshill Church of England Primary School.

1976

Graduates from Tutshill Primary and enrolls at Wyedean Comprehensive School.

1979

Learns about Jessica Mitford from Great-aunt Ivy.

1980

Anne Rowling diagnosed with multiple sclerosis (MS).

1982

Jo voted Head Girl during Year 11 at Wyedean Comprehensive.

1983

Graduates from Wyedean with honors and enrolls at Exeter University.

1985

Travels to Paris to study French and teach English.

1987

Graduates from Exeter and gets job as research assistant at Amnesty International.

1990

Stranded on a train in the English countryside, Rowling has vision of Harry Potter; starts outlining and sketching book series; Anne Rowling dies.

1991

Leaves Manchester to teach English in Oporto, Portugal.

1992

Marries Jorge Arantes.

1993

Gives birth to daughter, Jessica; separates from Arantes; returns to Britain; joins sister in Edinburgh, Scotland.

1994

Goes on welfare; lives in mouse-infested flat; tells Di about Harry Potter; writes in cafés around town.

1995

Completes *Harry Potter and the Philosopher's Stone*; types manuscript; searches for a literary agent; enrolls in a teaching credential program.

1996

Christopher Little Literary Agency accepts Rowling as client; Bloomsbury Publishing accepts the manuscript for publication; Rowling gains her teaching credential.

1997

Receives a grant from Scottish Arts Council to complete *Harry Potter and the Chamber of Secrets*; *Harry Potter and the Philosopher's*

Stone is published in Britain; Scholastic pays $105,000 for U.S. rights.

1998

Harry Potter and the Chamber of Secrets is published in Britain; *Harry Potter and the Sorcerer's Stone* is published in the United States.

1999

Harry Potter and the Prisoner of Azkaban is published in the United Kingdom and the United States; the book goes to number one on British best-seller lists; the first three books by Rowling hold the top three positions on the *New York Times* best-seller list; Warner Bros. wins the rights to make Harry Potter films.

2000

Harry Potter and the Goblet of Fire is published simultaneously in the United Kingdom and the United States in record first printings, becomes fastest-selling book of all time.

2001

Publishes *Quidditch Through the Ages* and *Fantastic Beasts and Where to Find Them*; the motion picture version of *Harry Potter and the Sorcerer's Stone* is released and becomes the top-grossing movie of the year; Rowling marries Dr. Neil Murray.

2002

Announces she is expecting her second child; hosts a Halloween ball at Stirling Castle to raise money for the MS Society Scotland; donates about £500,000 ($925,000) to the University of Aberdeen to create an MS research group.

2003

Gives birth to her second child, David Gordon Rowling Murray; *Harry Potter and the Order of the Phoenix* is released around the world, shattering all first-day sales records set by its predecessor; Rowling becomes the first author to attain a net worth of $1 billion; film version of *Harry Potter and the Chamber of Secrets* is released.

2004

Film version of *Harry Potter and the Prisoner of Azkaban* released; Rowling announces she is expecting her third child; Rowling completes manuscript of *Harry Potter and the Half-Blood Prince*.

2005

Gives birth to her third child, Mackenzie Jean Rowling Murray; *Harry Potter and the Half-Blood Prince* is released worldwide; *Harry Potter and the Goblet of Fire* motion picture is released.

2006

Announces she will finish the final book in the Harry Potter series in 2006; *Harry Potter and the Half-Blood Prince* named Book of the Year at the British Book Awards; Rowling funds substantial portion of £2.1 million grant made to Edinburgh University by the MS Society Scotland; Warner Bros. announces the motion picture version of *Harry Potter and the Order of the Phoenix* will be released on July 13, 2007.

For Further Reading

Books

George W. Beahm, *Fact, Fiction, and Folklore in Harry Potter's World: An Unofficial Guide*. Charlottesville, VA: Hampton Roads, 2005. A treasury of information about the history, myths, and legends woven through the Harry Potter series.

————, *Muggles and Magic: J.K. Rowling and the Harry Potter Phenomenon*. Charlottesville, VA: Hampton Roads, 2004. A collection of Harry Potter trivia and analysis, including a glossary of terms from the world of the boy wizard. Includes essays about Rowling's life and reviews of her work.

Lindsey Fraser, *Conversations with J.K. Rowling*. New York: Scholastic, 2000. J.K. Rowling's memories and musings presented in a question-and-answer format. This book contains reproductions of the author's whimsical line drawings, brief synopses of her books, and snippets of interviews with various magazines.

Connie Ann Kirk, *J.K. Rowling: A Biography*. Westport, CT: Greenwood, 2003. Part biography and part literary analysis, with a heavy emphasis on the latter. Includes discussions of the influence of other fantasy writers on Rowling and the world she has created.

Periodicals

Raffaela Barker, "Harry Potter's Mum," *Good Housekeeping*, October 2000.

Maureen Dowd, "Veni, Vidi, Voldemort," *New York Times*, December 9, 2001.

Eddie Gibb, "Tales from a Single Mother," *Times* (London), June 29, 1997.

Nancy Gibbs, "Harry Is an Old Soul," *Time*, December 25, 2000–January 1, 2001.

Elizabeth Gleick, "The Wizard of Hogwarts," *Time*, April 12, 1999.

Paul Gray, The Magic of Potter, *Time*, December 25, 2000–January 1, 2001.

Geordie Greig, "Special JK," *Tatler*, February 2006.

Malcolm Jones, "The Return of Harry Potter!" *Newsweek*, July 10, 2000.

William Plummer and Joanna Blonska, "Spell Binder," *People*, July 12, 1999.

Carla Power, "A Literary Sorceress," *Newsweek*, December 7, 1998.

Internet Sources

CBC "Interview: J.K. Rowling," *This Morning Sunday Edition*, October 23, 2000. http://radio.cbc.ca/programs/thismorning/sites/books/rowling_001023.html.

J.K. Rowling's interview with Amazon.co.uk. www.cliphoto.com/potter/interview.htm.

Harry Potter Galleries, "BarnesandNoble Chat Transcript," Barnesandnoble.com March 19, 1999. http://history.250x.com/vaults/c105.htm.

Web Sites

J.K. Rowling Official Site (www.jkrowling.com). Created by the author as a way to communicate with her fans, Rowling's official site includes biographical material, diary entries, unused fragments from the books, and much more.

The Leaky Cauldron (www.the-leaky-cauldron.org). The leading fan site for all things related to Harry Potter includes transcripts of news articles, links to news stories, fan essays, interviews with Rowling, merchandise, quizzes, games and more.

"Meet J.K. Rowling," Scholastic.com, (www.scholastic.com/harrypotter/author/index.htm). The American publisher of Rowling's books offers information about the author. Includes transcripts of interviews with Rowling.

A widely published poet and playwright, Bradley Steffens is the author of twenty-eight nonfiction books for children and young adults. His book *Giants* won the San Diego Book Award for best children's nonfiction book of 2005. He lives in Escondido, California, with his wife, Angela; stepson, John; and twin sons, Bryan and Brayden.